D1460988

THE GREAT BIKE RIDE

THE GREAT BIKE RIDE
(Around the World in 80 Days)

NICK SANDERS

Ashford Press Publishing
Southampton
1988

Published by   Ashford Press Publishing 1988
                1 Church Road
                Shedfield
                Hampshire SO3 2HW

British Library Cataloguing in Publication Data

Sanders, Nicholas
        The great bike ride
        Journeys round the world by bicycle – Personal observations
        I. Title
        910.4'1

        ISBN 1-85253-096-0

Cover design by Jordan and Jordan, Fareham
Book design by Jenny Liddle, Poole
Typeset by ImagePlus, Lewes
Printed and bound by Hartnolls Ltd, Bodmin

For Viv and John

CONTENTS

ACKNOWLEDGEMENTS

SPAR Sponsored the adventure and thanks are due to Mr Ray Tucker, Marketing Director. I am grateful to : David Charlton, then of Granard Communications and Cressy Leggatt; Janet Keen Johnstone of Hilton International; Harry, Jean and Graham Hall for supplying the bike, and the late Stephen Hall for assembling it brilliantly; Specialized Equipment for the accessories; Raleigh for the training bike; Lada for the UK back-up vehicle and Rob Roberts for the driving; Caradice for the panniers; Virgin Airlines for the flight from New York; Air New Zealand in Sydney; David Brown and Maddie Wiltshire for supporting the adventure on the *Saturday Picture Show*, Laurie Brown and David Walker for fixing my knee; Roger Schlesinger and Sara Fisher for supporting the book; Chris Bridge and Nicky Holford for helping edit the book, with special thanks to Jane Bannister; Viv Bouchier and her husband John for their tremendous and loyal friendship; Dad, for being there and for telling me that there is more substance in dreams than casual conversation.

And away I go!

1 · THE CHALLENGE

The world record was within my grasp. As I stood on the George Washington Bridge looking at Manhattan on the other side I was approaching my last few miles of cycling. After 78 days and more than 13,000 miles cycling around the world I knew I would break the record. I breathed deeply, and listened, straining to hear the call of New York. At that moment, I wanted most of all to convince myself that after the most gruelling days of my life my journey would have an end. The record was so nearly mine. Only the flight to London was needed to make the circumnavigation technically complete.

My breath mingled in the cold air with the exhaust fumes of a hundred cars. Each one hurled by more furiously than the last towards the skyline of a city filled with monstrous columns and modern-day turrets.

Surrounded by the cars, the wind, the noise, the dirt, the end, I was alone. I wanted to hear a sound that was familiar to give me comfort. But overriding the familiarity of New York was a much greater fear for I was returning to the world I had left behind for 78 days.

The bike rested on the giant steel cables of the bridge which at a distance had looked like a giant cobwebs. Now, standing so close, the concrete pillars that anchored those cables were the size of houses. The bridge looked battle-scarred and worn, not dissimilar to the state of the bike. The dust of a hot summer's crossing of America caked the brakes and scratches from errant flint and stray tarmac dug into the frame.

A wind whistled around those steel girders and I stood there, listless in the morning haze. I felt uneasy and sad. The journey had become everything to me and given me the security of knowing that each day would contain some element of consistency, the consistency of cycling twelve or more hours every day since July 25. Now it was September 19. I wondered what I would do when the project was over. As I stood in a daze my exhaustion began to drown any elation I might have had. In the distance, partly obscured by smog, the twin towers of the World Trade Centre rose out of Manhattan. I waited a moment, deciding how best to cross the Hudson River.

I could see workers on the way towards a factory where clouds of smoke emanated from its towering chimney. These clouds were born dirty. Some of the workers were black, others had the broad Grecian chins of men I'd seen hanging around the Greek villages in the early part of the adventure. The long-nosed ones sauntered like the youths under the columned streets of Bologna, except here their gait seemed more sullen. An Italian talked to me of his homeland as I waited at the base of the bridge.

'What did you think of Italy?' he asked.

'I flew across the Appenines between Bologna and Florence like a bird.' For a moment, the Italian's face alternated between wistfulness and pleasure as he recalled his own feelings of youth and freedom in these same mountains. I made a move. A traffic cop directed me to the Holland Tunnel which separated New York from New Jersey and I cycled into a city hanging dirty onto the edge of a continent. 'I can do it. It's so close to the record nothing must stop me now,' these words pounded forcefully through my mind as I got closer to the entrance of the tunnel.

Reaching New Jersey City's abandoned, dirty streets it was as if I'd left behind America the beautiful for America the garbage can. In America I had cycled across semi-arid deserts and mountain ranges, tediously forging across the flat plains of the mid-west. In the rest of the world there had been the plateaus of India and the rains of the Far East, the isolation of Australia and the long flight across the Pacific, jungles of extremes. Here was a different type of jungle. Waiting impatiently in the unmoving traffic I noticed graffiti-strewn red brick walls and burly cops who looked as if they regularly shovelled bits of bodies into black plastic bags. As the traffic moved slowly forward, I turned towards Manhattan.

Along Henderson Street, a right and a left and the tunnel entrance was directly ahead. Cycling across the bridge is not allowed and at the tunnel entrance bikes are forbidden. It appeared that it was actually going to be impossible to cycle legally all the way from Los Angeles to New York. So I waited for someone to take me through. A man in a van stopped and told me to 'jump in quick' and we rumbled underneath yellow strip lights. He told me, 'my wife's expecting our first baby tonight.' He looked so proud as we sidled alongside the World Trade Towers which were so tall it was not easy to see where they stopped.

'I've just cycled around the world,' I said.

'Then we've both achieved what we've wanted,' he replied, and we both threw our heads back and laughed

I wondered if there would be anyone to meet me. I reached the Hilton, my New York stopover, and climbing the steps, holding on to my bike, I turned around. Rushing and pushing along the crowded pavements everyone was in a hurry. Except for one man, who was leaning against the building. He waved his paper this way and that, swotting New York flies.

The feelings I had at the beginning of this journey came to me forcibly as I began to realise that the journey was at an end. What seemed such a long time ago I knew that in order to cycle around the world in 80 days, I would have to ride 171 miles a day whatever the weather or terrain. Since my first journey around the world at the age of twenty-three four years ago, I had cycled 50,000 miles through 45 countries. Without quite knowing why, such adventuring was to form the foundation for my attempt to 'race' around the world.

The real preparation began years ago in my teens. Every weekend was taken up with racing and I lived on the prizes I won from season to season. I was an amateur, and consequently was paid in kind, but the prize of a lightweight racing tyre could be sold for £5 which

would keep me going for perhaps four days. The sale of a case of cutlery could support me for a fortnight. After school, the local boys queued outside my bike shed, where, for a couple of hours I sold vital parts for bicycles, wrangling and bartering the best price for a pair of handlebars or brakes. Such income would add to the proceeds from my boxes of cutlery.

For most of my adolescent life I had been unconsciously working towards some goal without quite knowing what it was. In my late teens and early adult life, cycling had become a living. But now, for some inexplicable reason I began to realise there was something more that I wished to achieve. I wanted to cycle around the world more than anything I've ever wanted to do.

So in 1981, at the age of twenty-three, after eight years of scrambling around the race circuits of the UK and Europe, I had £400 in the bank and a bike which had been lent to me by a friend. With modest publicity and the generous backing of a local restaurant, I set off to cycle around the world and did so in 138 days, beating the world's previous best by five days. I required at least £1.50 a day to live and eat. I borrowed half from the bank and worked as a barman to secure the rest.

After 137 days I arrived in New York. It was July 4 and I crept out of America unobserved. The following morning I returned to my home town equally unnoticed. Britain was ablaze with the race riots of 1981. I had cycled around the world faster than anyone had ever dared and no-one was interested in my story. The journey was duly filed in the *Guinness Book of Records*.

My spring of '82 sweltered, slowly cycling the length of Sumatra amongst the swamps and the crocodiles. During the summer that same year I rode the periphery of Asia from Damascus to Singapore. My summer of '83 blistered, riding through Egypt, Sudan and Central Africa along the banks of the Nile until I eventually reached its source; 4,165 miles south of Cairo where the rainclouds tippled their load on a hillock not far from the shores of Lake Tanganyika in Burundi.

In 1984 I journeyed twice around the coastline of mainland Britain, each occasion undertaking an adventure lasting 4,802 miles. This was the second record I accumulated and it, too, was filed as before.

The possibility of a journey around the world in 80 days was inspired by the title of Jules Verne's legendary novel. Phileas Fogg and his servant Paspart-out set out by train and steamer to complete a journey thought impossible at the time. It was coincidental that 80 days divided the mileage of 13,608 miles I had made on the first journey into 171 miles cycling for each of those days, which I considered the limit of my capacity.

Sponsorship is a major factor in the success of a journey. The first five years of my adventuring were a balance between coming to an understanding of various commercial and promotional arrangements, and the need to separate the real objective of the journeys, the realisation of a personal dream. However, I learned early on that without deliberate publicity, the journeys would receive scant attention and the financing would be more difficult.

Several organisations had shown an interest in my project but by March, no money had been forthcoming. I was

becoming resigned to having to cycle around the world again on a very limited budget. There was no question of the journey being abandoned due to lack of finance. One afternoon I met up with a friend of mine, Frank Dickens. Frank was a cartoonist, drawing 'Bristow' for the *Evening Standard*. He still rode a bike well and was interested in helping me. He suggested I speak to a friend of his called Lucy who worked for Granard Communications, a public relations firm in the city. I wasn't very hopeful but gave her a few details. She in turn said she would pass her notes in a memo around the office to see if any of the other account directors could see a use for my adventure. I thanked Frank and went back to my rented room which acted as my office in Glossop. To my surprise, the very next day I received a phone call from David Charlton who liked the idea and thought Guinness would be perfect for such an international journey. He asked me how much I needed and I said £20,000. Two days later I was to hear that the proposal had been rejected.

I didn't really need this amount of money to ride around the world but I had a large overdraft to pay off and I couldn't think of any other way to do it. After my adventure to the source of the White Nile I decided to try and make my fortune in publishing and produced my first book myself. By investing my sponsors' money, selling copies in advance and borrowing heavily from the bank using the collatoral of a friend's mortgage, I secured enough finance to produce *Journey to the Source of the Nile* published by Nick Sanders Limited. The following year I rode around the coast of Britain twice in the pursuit of a record and the material for book number two. It, too, was produced in the wake of one financial crisis

after another, the culmination of which left me owing my creditors £26,000. My abilities as a businessman were similar to those I had shown as a barman: I spent more time chatting up the girls in the kitchen for any left over cream cakes than serving behind the bar. If I were to continue as an adventurer, as some sort of writer, in fact if I were to continue at all, another journey became essential to keep afloat.

Mentally and physically I was prepared and ready to undertake the journey that summer. BBC television's *Saturday Picture Show* was keen to broadcast phone calls and film sections of the journey and I knew instinctively that it was a good inspirational adventure which didn't have to be taken too seriously. Having tried numerous areas hoping to receive financial support, I waited, for whatever was to happen.

Two weeks after my first contact with David Charlton, he telephoned me again telling me that the *SPAR* food organisation were interested in what I had to offer and would I present myself to their Marketing Director, Ray Tucker. Four days later I met Ray who, to my surprise, was very excited about the whole idea and it was generally agreed it would fit well into their marketing campaign for the summer. A week later I met John Irish, the dynamic and exuberant Managing Director of *SPAR*, who praised the project and it was accepted. I was well and truly 'on the road'.

The bike was designed specially for me by Harry Hall, one of the most expert bicycle builders in the country. He had spent years refining and adjusting the shape of the frame. The complete bike weighed only 18 lb and being so light it lacked nothing in strength. The fourteen gears clicked smoothly and exactly; I would be able to select the most suitable gear ratio for whatever gradient I should encounter. The wheels were designed to ride over the roughest terrain and the few spare spokes I carried would correct any little damage that might occur. The angles of the frame were tailored to suit my body perfectly, so, for example, the position of the seat in relation to the handlebars was exactly right. If the wheelbase or the length of the bike was too long, my back and arms would be stretched uncomfortably and I would be less efficient. If the wheelbase had been too short my body would be cramped, hunched over the handlebars and I would tire prematurely. I wasn't just cycling around the world, it was a race against time and the speed I would have to maintain to accumulate such a large daily mileage would allow for no error in judgement or design. Small panniers on the front of the bike counterbalanced me at the back. I would use the minimum of equipment, and the reduction in weight would aid my speed tremendously. I carried only a passport, money, a camera, a mini-tape recorder, a diary, a book of maps, one spare tee-shirt and shorts, a sleeping bag, three spanners, a repair kit, two tyres, and two inner tubes: *nothing* else. Food I would have to buy from roadside restaurants and water would be sipped from streams. Even across the most barren parts of this particular route, I would never be further than a day's ride from sustenance.

I needed to be very fit, perhaps fitter than ever before. I would have to be able to ride to the top of a ten-mile mountain, recover on the following descent in readiness for any subsequent ascents that might follow; day after day. To withstand daily extremes of temperature from a frosty morning to a 40°C mid-day sun I needed to be physically very efficient. In the event of a tumble and serious grazing I had to be tough enough to get back on my bike straight away as if nothing had happened. To make all this possible I intended to prepare by cycling 10,000 miles between January and the end of April 1985. Mentally, I did not allow myself a single negative thought. Everything had to be done to give me the greatest chance of capturing a world record that might last a very long time.

When the equipment was organised and the training well under-way, I turned my attention to the bureaucratic part of the adventure, such as obtaining visas for Syria, Jordan, Egypt, Australia and America. Also I had to ascertain what constituted a journey around the world. The *Guinness Book of Records* said it was partly a matter of commonsense, but should take into consideration that there was a minimum around the world road distance of approximately 10,000 miles and that I should travel through several continents in an easterly or westerly direction. Also I had to beat, in time and distance, any previous record.

As the weeks passed, I pored over maps of the Middle East, India and the Malay Peninsula. I suspected that these areas of the world would be less well sign posted than Europe, Australasia and America and so I would have to be absolutely sure of my route. Everything had to be right. Nothing could be overlooked or left to chance. Money would be forwarded and waiting for me in various banks. Correspondence would be sent to hotels on route. So that nothing would be forgotten, I telephoned my sponsors nearly every day to discuss things. Journalists from newspapers and radio stations began to enquire about the journey, and the *Saturday Picture Show* started to make arrange-

6

ments to film me in various parts of the world. I started to feel a little pressured by such activity, but fortunately Vivienne, a friend who assisted me with all my correspondence, helped organize the publicity.

The fine details of the journey were not easy for me. I was full of ideas. I don't like the mundane routine of ordinary life. Yet in a twist of circumstance, cycling around the world was simply an extension of the ordinariness I didn't like.

My training was progressing well. Three thousand miles into the middle of February, I had overcome my initial lack of fitness. Five thousand miles into March and I was halfway there. I could easily cycle 100 miles without appearing out of breath. My heart beat regularly and strongly as I tested myself over the most extreme Pennine climbs. By April showers, my aching legs had cycled 7,500 miles. Now I could ride 150 miles in ten hours however inclement the weather. My body was lean and efficient. In the snow and the rain I felt warm; in the warmth of a rare sunny spring morning I perspired just enough to keep cool, wasting as little body fluid as possible. I lived alone on purpose for a solitary attitude had also to be strengthened. Once the journey started I would be alone and it would be easier not to think of family and friends too often. For this reason, I rented two rooms over a hairdresser's shop in Glossop, going out to train at 9 a.m., and returning around 4 p.m. In one of the rooms I lived and worked, in the other I washed away the day's grit in an old square porcelain sink. As the weeks passed I felt harder and stronger, my confidence increased and the pressure of the publicity was easier to withstand. I was keen, resolute, toned and ready to go.

But something was wrong. My left knee had begun to ache. I continued training in spite of the little pain. All the last minute details had been sorted out; television coverage, radio phone calls, overseas accommodation and flights from continent to continent booked wherever possible; it was just a matter of staying upright on the bike. But soon the knee became immobile and one morning before Easter I woke up clutching it with both hands.

With less than four weeks to go I knew something was seriously wrong. I was panic-stricken. I couldn't walk. My psyched-up, heightened mental preparations couldn't cope with this. I sought the best treatment possible which led me to ex-Manchester United physiotherapist Laurie Brown, now with the England cricket team. If he couldn't fix me up I would despair.

Laurie could see that I was depressed. He told me the training had been too hard, and that I needed rest. I knew that would cause a delay. The knee was probably only inflamed and while knees are usually quick to heal, there was no certainty about when I would be able to continue.

April 7th Trouble with the knee
The physiotherapy has started in earnest. The ultra-sound machine sends high frequency waves into torn knee ligaments which I am told is the latest type of treatment. Laurie seems to know I'm on the point of panicking. Twenty-Five days before the start it doesn't look hopeful. The feeling of despair is total. I don't want to believe that there is something seriously wrong with the knee or that the trip will have to be cancelled.

Laurie was certainly right. Time alone would have made me well. But to speed up the process he introduced me to David Walker, a consultant orthopaedic surgeon. On Easter Sunday David gave me my first cortisone injection. 'Nothing more serious than a damaged synovial membrane,' he said. Shortly after, I managed to cycle 200 yards before doubling up with pain.

Both Laurie Brown and David Walker had decided I should have a small operation. If I couldn't climb stairs I knew for sure cycling would be impossible. As I was being wheeled in for my 'pre-med', I felt apprehensive as the anaesthetic took effect.

In my mind, days now were numbers and a dream I had was distorted by baobab trees and elephants, which were positioned on the side of the road as mile posts, and they marked time on the side of the road, waiting for me to go past. I heard screaming in the distance, it was muffled as if in a tunnel. Slowly the screams became recognisable as those from a person, and getting close to me they were louder. Normally such a nightmare would wake me up, now I was unable to shake myself free from the vile sounds of such a dreadful dream. These images were very abstract and the vague picture of the journey had become a hallucination. For one fleeting moment I wondered how I might feel if, once the journey began, the hallucination was still there.

2 · THE BEGINNING

Day 1: July 6

All is quiet outside but inside me there is a lot of noise. The turmoil around me is closing in and the original idea is now an obsession bordering on stage-fright.

The project had to be postponed for a month, and the new starting date was July 6. Two weeks rest after the operation seemed to have allowed the inflammation to heal and I hadn't lost too much of my fitness. The journey would have to start more slowly than I'd intended and any time lost from the schedule would have to be made up later. My passport was in order, bags packed, and the bicycle gleaming, a new press release was issued, and I began my attempt to accomplish something that I wasn't sure was possible.

It was a strange feeling on *Day 1* that propelled me through the suburbs of Manchester. I said goodbye and thanked everybody, bystanders, friends and press, who gave me such a warm send-off. There must have been thirty or forty people, all taking photographs, and all shouting to me to hurry home soon. Some of the bystanders I didn't know, but there were faces from the *Manchester Evening News*, Piccadilly Radio and Radio Manchester who I'd become acquainted with dur-

ing my years of adventuring. The *Picture Show* were there as well as Look North West television and for a few moments it was all very exciting. I had already said goodbye to my Dad, but, in the back of the crowd, I knew he would already be waiting for my return. Cycling in the direction of the Cheshire plain, it was just possible I had forgotten someone. It was too late now. Setting off, I intended to savour today's moment of glory for a few miles. It would be a while before it happened again, if it ever did. More to the point, it was raining. It was an inauspicious start.

Along the Macclesfield Road I smiled at my earlier panic. 'When you're cycling distances it is easier to look at something that doesn't move' other cyclists say, 'start off looking at cows before you look at things that fly'. Sweeping past sun-tinted houses and their brightly coloured porches, the countryside brushed me in slow motion. I unwrapped a sheet of heavily waxed greaseproof paper and pulled out a ham sandwich the shape of a door wedge.

Calling today Day 1 seemed strange now it was happening. Perhaps it was my 'pre-med' dream continuing unresolved. It was in this way that I passed the arabesque turrets of Capesthorne Hall. Before my elation disappeared, I

had passed through Stoke on Trent and was close to Birmingham. The wind was blowing a gale, and the long straight road that was all important raced beneath me. Often, when I was younger, my Dad told me he saw roads like this, except his roads, he said, wound between sheep and peat bogs immersed in a silence broken only by the 'kowk-ok-ok' of the crowing grouse. Long since retired, he had worked in factories, rebelled as a youth, owned newspaper shops and lost them. An enlightened man, he harboured not a trace of bitterness, 'what is lost,' he would say, 'is not worth having'.

The pedalling became more rhythmic as the day's fatigue made the effort automatic, I knew too, that the act of cycling would soon take over whatever else the body hoped to do. As the day proceeded and the fatigue increased, the altered awareness to pain became more precise. At a certain point, the fatigue is such that you cannot continue however hard you try. Sipping tea out of a big mug in a café not far from Rugby, I wondered if they would serve tea like this on the other side of the world.

Long summer nights enticed people onto the streets of England as I cycled down to London. Families grouped and chatted whilst lovers whispered sensuous thoughts. Boys and girls kicked footballs along side streets, their shouts of anger and glee bursting through the quiet evening.

On and on I cycled and I remembered Dad boasting of a long summer night when he cycled the return journey of 190 miles from Manchester to Llandudno to Manchester. 'There and back in eleven hours, and not even out of breath.' He put down his pint of home brew and looked very serious, 'and I only had one gear'.

I was now ready to leave the shores of my own country. I was ready to strive for this rather strange quest, to break a world record few people had ever heard off. I thought of the miles, the days on the road, the times it would hurt. I thought of Dad, because I knew he would be thinking of me.

That evening I slept soundly in my sleeping bag in a field a little north of Luton, having ridden 140 miles since 1 p.m. If I was to keep to my schedule, by tomorrow I had to ride the 100 miles to Dover, cross the Channel, and try to and reach Amsterdam by evening.

Day 2: Crossing the Channel

Crossing a sea can give a sense of real terror, of excitement. Already a battle is welling up inside me. Part of me wants to go on, to stand before every new experience and absorb whatever might happen; part wants to return home and never stray away from what I know. But deep inside, I know that whatever should happen, I can never be the same again.

It was a bit chilly sitting on the top deck of the ferry, but the sun was shining and any apprehension I had was tempered by the relief of being on the way to breaking a world record. It must have been around 11 a.m. as seagulls screeched and littered the sky and quite suddenly I remembered reading something from the American poet Walt Whitman:

'I heard what was said of the universe
Heard it and heard it of several
    thousand years,
It is middling well as far as it goes – but
    is that all?'

If there was any reason at all for a jour-

ney like this, then discovering whether the universe is middling well I'm sure would do.

The sea rushed and beat the side of the ferry while a couple of youths sat next to me holding hands. I casually glimpsed an angular-featured boy sitting beside the beautiful profile of a very pretty face. I saw a most beautiful woman and feeling self conscious in my shorts and pale English legs, hoped she wouldn't notice me. The couple were quite oblivious of everyone until, turning around, the girl asked me something I didn't even hear properly.

'Would you like a can of beer? We've bought too many duty frees'

If I hadn't made a conscious effort to control it, my face would have crumpled in dismay. The other side of that wonderfully paintable, statuesque form appeared to be too large for her head and hung in elephant folds from forehead to chin. Her right eye hung rheumy, whilst the other side of those lips sagged heavily. I marvelled at the courage needed to overcome such deformity.

'It's my twenty-first birthday today,' she told me, 'and we're celebrating.' She looked away for a moment and then carried on, 'I haven't been out of my room properly until now.' We drank a can of beer each in silence. I didn't know what to say. Turning to speak she stared at me, determined, I thought, to hold my gaze.

'How do I look?'

'Beautiful,' I said. My throat tightened and my eyes watered. Weeping would have been easier than talking. I couldn't speak another word. Just then a fellow sat down next to her, he had a swastika tattooed on the tip of his nose and a spider's web around his neck.

'This is my boyfriend.' She gently put her arm around him. 'Look what he did for me.' She showed me his face scarred by compass scratches, filled in with a ball point pen. To mark the emergence of his lady he decided it was the only gesture he could make. 'Yeh, he did this just for me.' Pulling him towards her face, very softly she kissed him. As I sat watching, I felt ashamed for I had no idea that such a love could exist.

The ferry began to clunk and whirr and less than a couple of hours away from Britain we were now attached to Belgium. I wheeled my bike out of the carhold, and met a couple of journalists on the other side of customs. It was sunny in Belgium. We chatted about the journey and whether breaking the record was possible. The ferry sounded its horn as if to send me on my way. Winding past a boat-sprinkled harbour I reached the road to Amsterdam quickly. A few left-over tulips blew in the same direction as me and the wind; and the afternoon was as fresh as cut grass. A car hooted and as I moved over to let it pass, and the girl from the boat leaned out of a brand new black Mercedes. Shouting good luck, she threw me an orange and she waved and shouted and laughed until the car disappeared out of sight.

Not quite sure where I was going, I asked a policeman for directions to Amsterdam.

'Amsterdam, eh?' he said.

'Yes, officer, Amsterdam.'

Muttering to himself he churned the word around a bit and put his hands on his hips. 'So you want to go to Amsterdam?' he said slowly, raising his eyebrows, 'it is very far.'

'Well I'm cycling around the world you see,' I said, just to confuse him, 'so it's not really that far.'

'Ja, around the world, ja, that is good.' He pushed his hat to the back of his head. Continuing the journey in any direction I reckoned would be more profitable than waiting for this policeman to come up with anything positive. Politely I said I was in a hurry and saying goodbye I left him, standing there with his arms folded.

It took all morning and early afternoon to pedal through the West Flanders region of Belgium; past the medieval town of Bruges, a sharp left at Ghent and across the cobbled city centre of Antwerp where Rubens painted. My Belgian experience lasted for 70 miles and four hours before I crossed the border into Holland. It was still *Day 2* and it seemed crazy that I was already in Holland and that tomorrow I should be in Germany. As if to break me gently into the ride the wind was behind me, pushing me north, past Breda, across the River Maas, Utrecht and I was gliding along with the sun burning my left hand side. The flat miles to Amsterdam were completed eight hours after disembarking from the ferry.

That night I was to sleep in the Hilton. They were one of my sponsors and were to look after me in various cities. As I arrived at the hotel I was assured by the doorman that the bike would be wheeled through the foyer and taken immediately to my room. A young man calling himself Front Desk Manager cordially greeted me and suggested I might like to freshen up. At 8 p.m. precisely three Dutch journalists would be dining with me, so I had 15 minutes to rest, bath, change my clothes and present myself. Compared to the less than salubrious establishments in which I usually stay, the lift that took me to the twelfth floor would have been more than suitable accommodation. However, I was to have a room of my own.

Suitably attired in my entire social

wardrobe of three items; shirt, trousers and plimsols, I headed for a sizeable plate of steak and chips. I was introduced to three men, all older than myself. Charles had grey hair and a long face. He looked intelligent, though his expression was only prevented from being dour by his smiling eyes. Smoking a cigarette from a short black holder he introduced himself and his colleagues Nico and Paul.

'Enchanted,' said Nico taking a deep bow. 'We have been awaiting your arrival with some suspense.' His eyes glinted. Charles and Paul were a little less demonstrative and as they shook my hand limply while Nico hid his face behind the menu.

Certainly they seemed a little out of the ordinary, and the tone of their conversation proved quite eccentric. But it at least gave my conversation-starved brain some human stimulation.

'You are thinking,' Nico said to me, peering over the top of his menu, 'you ought to eat your chips and not think. It is easier that way.' He had unmoving black eyes that gave nothing away. I was simply looking around for a welcoming glance, but this fellow withstood any advance from anyone. His cheeks were full and hung around a face that had just enough wrinkles to dispel images of an easy life.

'I don't like your cycle paths,' I said trying to make conversation. 'I really need my freedom to ride anywhere.'

'Cycle path?' Nico looked at Charles puzzled.

'Ah! Psychopath,' Charles translated, 'you are going to be a mad killer?'

'Yes,' said Nico, 'when this journey is over you will go mad and kill yourself, after all, what else is there to do?'

Paul, who was altogether more predictable, hung grimly on to a pint of lager and attempted a few questions.

'You see, you are late and how shall I say, we have enjoyed the warmness of a quiet evening drink as we sit bathed in moonlight.'

'Moonlight, bosh,' said Nico, 'you are too sentimental and must not be listened to.'

'Are you sentimental?' Charles asked me.

'Occasionally.'

'I am often, and now I should like to weep.'

I asked him why, but he said nothing. He certainly looked sad with that long, melancholy face.

'The poor dear misses his dog,' said Nico, playing at being magnanimous, and directing my attention away from his woeful friend. 'Come, we must eat away our sorrows.' Pausing to pick and stab at a rather large lobster, he puckered his lips at Charles. 'He is such a darling and so are you.' With that he left the lobster alone and blew us a kiss.

'Stop this,' Charles implored whilst his eyes smiled. 'You will give this chap crap, or as we say in China, clap.'

The meal was good and the company bizarre. If I had been to places one only dreams about, these cynical, scrambled, paranoiac, mad, alienist screwballs had been there before me. What could these journalists write about me that they didn't know already? I felt that I was full of the hope they no longer had.

'I used to be a skipper,' Nico said quite unexpectedly, 'of an old tub in the Indian Ocean.' He raised his arms with a theatrical gesture. 'Yes, I was, how do you say, rubbing the shoulders with the debris of life, and in the end I married a Turkish princess.'

'What, a little Turkish delight?' I said slightly facetiously.

'She was not a delight,' Nico thundered back, making me jump in my seat, 'she was a Turkish whore and if I ever set eyes on her again I'll kill her.' The other journalists were obviously used to Nico ranting about this Turkish woman, he seemed a little mad to me.

'My parents wanted me to come home, to leave Istanbul, and she wouldn't let me. When I did get home they were dead, a plane crash the weekend before.'

'I know how you must feel,' I said, and looking down at my meal fell silent. I remembered the death of my own mother. Cycling through Uganda and returning from the source of the Nile I knew I would never see her again. When I arrived in Cairo a letter awaited me. It was the one letter of my life which in order to discover its contents I knew did not need opening. I wanted so much to return to her, triumphant from my journeying, and hold her hand just for a few moments more and tell her as she died what I was unable to do as she lived, that I loved her. But helpless in a foreign land, I could be perversely thankful that separated from her pain and miserable dissolution from life, I would try and not believe what I could not see. Yet, even though I knew that my source of understanding had control over my heart, I also knew that the exorcism of my own mother would never be complete. I looked up to see Nico staring at me.

'And so you put on a brave face and continue?' 'In life there is only one choice,' Nico said sombrely, 'in death there are no choices, and so for reasons that elude me now, I became an actor portraying the less conventional aspects of life, and with a little inheritance spent huge sums of money drinking with my friend Charles. Now I am a journalist which is the same as an actor and this is why we are here to talk to you.'

Charles in the meantime returned from the telephone.

'He has telephoned his wife,' Nico informed me, pausing, 'to speak to his dog' and without a glimmer of a smile could see I didn't understand. 'He loves his dog more than his wife and likes to hear him bark, so he asks his wife to bring the dog to the phone. She pulls his tail and he barks.' Charles did look happy with his rather sickly immovable smile. 'Ah well, my darling,' Nico said to me, 'what is that English proverb, you know, the one that says "it is better to have loved a dog than never to have loved at all."'

Day 3: One day across Holland.
The journey is two days old and although 80 days doesn't seem such a long time, I feel day by day it will take an eternity. As yet I have no sense of urgency. I cannot imagine how my journey will shape up. At the moment I am concentrating heavily on the sheer physical effort needed to remain near to that schedule of 170 miles each day. When I am fitter and the pedalling becomes a little easier, maybe I will be able to stop and look around.

The next day was sunny, and as ribbons and taffeta flapped from the pony tails of little girls walking by the river bank, I sat under a sycamore tree. Holland celebrated Sunday morning with a bicycle ride and this side of the river was awash with bicycles. Sitting lazily while the sun-spangled river wound its ponderous way, I allowed myself 30 minutes to watch freshly-ironed shirts of old ladies and the bare knees of little boys. Peering through wire-rimmed glasses, the old ladies walked past and nodded stiffly.

I had imagined what it was like to sit underneath a sycamore tree under the stars, now I was doing just that. I was as confused as anyone who had considered cycling around the world. Why me? What had I done to deserve such dubious abilities that required me to do this journey in the first place? So, sitting under this extremely ordinary sycamore tree I waited for something extraordinary to happen. In the adventure books that I had read, seemingly every page was brimmed with pathos and stories of human interest that made your knuckles go white. Instead, I sat watching an old barge ply past, an old barge-lady pinning out her washing. Everything was too ordinary. Something was missing, all I wanted was a little tempest perhaps, a whale in the river, a coiled python maybe to drop on my head and swallow me whole; then I would really know I was having an adventure.

Gazing away from the river I saw, standing in front of me, a small round face sticking out a tongue. I liked this form of communication, it was easy to understand, so I stuck mine out as well. Mum scolded her awfully rude child and at the same time threw me a withering look. As I climbed on my bike and creaked into motion, I looked around and saw a nose being tugged away within which was stuffed a finger. Underneath both was a smile.

Somehow I had managed to find the road to Eindhoven. The route planning today was so imprecise that had I ended up on any other road, I would have probably followed that. As it happened Eindhoven was on my schedule so things were looking promising. In Holland, as I complained to Nico, you have to ride on cycle paths which usually wind through the most intricate of housing estates. One moment I knew exactly where I was going, the next I would be directed away from busy sections of road, winding away quite

cheerfully, but irretrievably lost. It was no wonder the fellow tending to his Butchers Broom dropped his pruning clippers when I passed for the fourth time. After a round-the-houses search for Utrecht, via two culs-de-sac and three bouts of paranioa, I eventually found the town of Houten. A little later came Coulemburg and, at last, I was back on the road to Eindhoven.

I was behind schedule. If I wanted to reach the German border that night, I would have to forgo all things Dutch, leave the cycle paths to the timid, and take to the road.

I had intended, during the first few days of the journey, to hone up on my last weeks of training. It was 600 miles to Austria and by then I hoped I would be as fit as a little flea. At that point, the record breaking business would commence in earnest. So far I was riding an average of 150 miles each day. Soon that would have to rise to 170, and occasionally 200 miles in a single day would have to be recorded somewhere in the latter quarter of the journey. Whenever I was able I asked people on the roadside to sign my diary and so testify that they had seen me and that I was cycling around the world. If I collected enough signatures spread out every few miles thoughout the day it would make it difficult to keep hopping on and off trains or lorries, still collect the evidence and still cover my average distance each day.

Rolling along briskly without a care in the world, I felt a fresh breeze, lively and invigorating. Suddenly I realised I had forgotten to buy guilders. It was Sunday and the banks would be closed. Instant gloom set in and as I pedalled jerkily forward, the wind turned bitter and quite chilly. I wondered what to do when a racing cyclist dashed past without a moment to spare. I could do worse than try to keep up with him. It would at least take my mind off a rumbling stomach. It took ages to catch him up, my panniers flapping in the wind.

Across the flat plains of the Gelderland the two of us charged; along the banks of the Neder-Rhine and past the tin smelters of Arnhem, my head bobbed from side to side. There is an optimum speed to see the scenery, but now the trees were rushing past faster than I could count. At 20 miles per hour, the journey took on quite a different meaning. Fields of electric red tulips were flashed onto my vision, but that was as far as they went. Time, distance and objectives were all narrowed down to keeping up with this cyclist. Along the cycle paths, then the road, we weaved through villages, stopping only once for water. I was shattered, and Helmut, as the fellow was called, invited me home to accept a little Dutch hospitality. After a whole afternoon seeing little other than Helmut's back wheel, we finally pushed our bikes into a small back garden. His mother brought out a tray of tea and cakes and I munched hungrily, slurping tea as she watched my every move.

'More tea, Vicar?' I said to Helmut.

'Ah yes, of course,' he paused, 'but what is this wicker?'

'Oh, just a silly English joke.'

He dashed off to fill the teapot. The cakes were nice but the tea was horrible.

'You don't like tea? I checked the dictionary for your word thicker, make tea thicker, ja, double the measure?'

I was asked in faltering English if I liked Holland. I hadn't seen any clogs or windmills, so I would write home that the Dutch bake lovely cakes but make awful tea. What else could I say? Goodbye. Pedalling at a gentler pace into early evening shadows, I relieved myself of Helmut's tea at the first given opportunity.

'Hey you, no, no, no.'

Startled, I looked around. A policeman from across the road was beckoning me to stop what I was doing, but I couldn't. Too much disgusting tea. As he walked towards me, I fastened myself up, leaped on my bike and pedalled quickly out of harm's way.

Within a couple of hours I was sitting in a café on the border town of Velno. The proprietor accepted a German mark for a cup of coffee which I sipped slowly at the bar. Fixed in between a pair of carved mahoghany pillars, a large mirror reflected most of the customers. Examining every wrinkle I screwed up my face. I laughed at the ridiculousness of the situation. What I was doing was completely absurd. In the mirror I saw the pouting lips of a paper-doll face turn towards me and snigger. A yellow ribbon tied her hair into a top knot which matched a lemon coloured dress. Everyone in the bar stared at me in such a mean way that I began to feel uncomfortable. The bellies of these men pressed against the bar and short fat arms cradled glasses of beer. A man with black teeth turned his back toward me and farted and a companion choked, laughing, froth dripping like frogspawn from his beard. I knew I wasn't the only absurd person in the world, so I drank my coffee, slowly and deliberatly and then left. It was 10 p.m. and, finding a field where I would be safely hidden, I closed my eyes.

17

3 · ACROSS EUROPE

Day 4: From Holland to Germany.
Everything feels so ordinary, this journey is not the journey of my dreams. I imagined every day would be colourful and exciting. What I failed to imagine accurately was the tedious repetition necessary each day to cycle enough miles to remain on schedule. I seem to be cycling all the time with hardly a moment to consider anything else.

The following morning I rode through the empty lamplit streets of Münchengladbach. Around the corner in Neuss lived one of the passions of my teenage life, Anke Knoffleberger. Any other name couldn't have been more suitable and she looked puzzled whenever she squeezed every last breath out of my body. Built like a battleship, she possessed the sensuality of a marching army. Her heart, however, was in the right place, situated as it was somewhere in between shoulders nearly four foot wide. She called me her 'little destroyer,' and how she picked me up playfully during those balmy summer nights of '76. I wanted to telephone her, but she would be bigger now, and probably a health hazard to anyone under seven foot tall. I decided not to render the memory of her imperfect by our meeting, so rode quickly on to Düsseldorf.

Industrial Germany clogged up my hair, my eyes, my lungs and chemically cracked my lips. Squashed between curling wisps of yellow smoke and office blocks whose mirror windows reflected a dirty sun, tractors trundled up and down the Rhine floodplain, easing their way through rows of cabbages and turnips. In the Ruhr Valley there seemed to be very defined levels of life. Fighter jets struck past Jumbo 747's, which in turn drowned out the sound of the Düsseldorf-Köln Express. Speeding cars overtook belching lorries, which overtook creaking trams overtaking me. Electricity pylons stood like fence poles holding cables that seemed to form a net. In what looked like chaos, I carried on cycling, thinking that only the most invisible of people slip through the confines of such a zoo.

I dreaded cycling through cities in Germany. Each time one appeared I lost valuable hours, battling my way through a plethora of seemingly redundant directions. Cities are like that, but I didn't expect too bad a problem this side of India. The 80-day record was not as yet a really major consideration, I was not yet racing against time but I had to speed up my progress. This part of Germany was one of the most industrialised areas in the world. For me it became a wilderness. It was as if I'd been cycling for weeks between workshops and polluted rivers, my only glimpse of countryside being waving heads of hay between factory walls.

By early afternoon I had cycled for eight hours. That would work out at around 120 miles, another 50 miles and I would reach my day's quota. Brick walls and chimneys were gradually diluted by green fields and rolling hills. Winding between hawthorn and dogwood, the road was not long and straight, but still I could pedal and think.

Before I left England, the world record meant everything to me. Right now, the meaning of cycling around the world in 80 days was lost. Such a little bicycle fighting to get round such a big world wasn't a fair battle. The horizon stretched in every direction. How could I know the world was round and that I was to go *around* it?

Later that afternoon I reached Leverkusen. By tea-time I sat in a café in Altenkichen, in the evening I ate pizza in a restaurant in the old town of Limburg. These places were just names to me in the same way that days were becoming numbers. Each day I cycled; ate chips; drank tea and slept in fields. I also crossed very different countries in rapid succession; saw a thousand new faces; thought a hundred new thoughts.

Day 5: On the road to Frankfurt
Woke up at 5 a.m. after an uncomfortable night's sleep in a soggy field. Sometimes I ride far into the night and become so tired, it's easier not to book into a hotel and just unpack my sleeping bag and climb in fully clothed. All I have to do when day breaks is pack it up again and carry on for another 12 or 14 hours.

By breakfast time I was sitting in the city centre of Frankfurt drinking tea.

Whenever I sat down for a few minutes my legs would cramp and cease to move. Only by massaging them was I be able to straighten them, slowly, by degrees, until eventually I could stand and mount my bike. I couldn't imagine what the people of Frankfurt thought as they saw me hunched over my knees rubbing them furiously. With legs that now worked I eventually rode on to Selingenborg. Further along I stopped and sat quietly on the banks of the Main, the little town of Marktheidenfeld signalled the end of today's effort. A whole day had disappeared and the only thing I could remember was my knee massage in Frankfurt. From what I remembered of the first bike ride around the world four years ago, it was surely more exciting than this. I freewheeled down a narrow cobbled street and parked my bike outside a small tavern advertising '*brotwurst*'. The lady serving behind the bar had the most exquisite cheekbones and beautiful long black hair. Sitting down by the window where I could watch my bike I ordered a plate of sausage and chips. By the table next to mine, a young couple were clutching each other with an embrace so full of passion they sat locked together. The sausage and chips arrived, the only kind of comfort I was going to get tonight.

'They're always at it,' the bar lady said to me, 'I don't know where they get the energy from.'

'I've not seen them breathe yet,' I said in astonishment.

'Oh, they don't breathe,' she said as if it were a matter of fact, 'they just take a deep breath and hope for the best.'

She told me she was from Amsterdam and that she'd been here these past four years.

'Germans are all the same,' she said quietly, standing a little closer, 'intense.' So close, I noticed her lips, the most curved I had ever seen. She was very beautiful and I so much wanted to tell her so, but couldn't.

The chips were good. After fifteen years of eating little else, I regarded myself as something of a connossieur. Carving up my enormously long sausage, I became aware again of the couple next to me. They were still at it, in a fit of frenzy. It would seem that the only alternative view of the universe these people were going to get this evening was the inside of each other's nostrils. Perhaps not such a bad compromise. The lady from behind the bar may have

had the softest of complexions, the gentlest of natures, the sweetest of smells, but time gave me no choice but to glimpse. I would end this journey with a saddlebag full of glimpses from all over the world. That night I slept on the outskirts of Würzburg, and the next night I settled down under a rhododendron bush somewhere a little north of Munich.

The sweet smell of sawn timber and cut grass overpowered the first minutes of the next day. As shafts of hay, more red than yellow, wafted, Sunday morning sounds of tolling bells echoed down the valley. By breakfast time I had been

21

on the road for three hours. North of Munich the roads were quiet. I had now completed one sixteenth of the journey and until this morning I hadn't been conscious of my own tyres on the road. There appeared to be two types of whooshing; one for the tarmac, one for the white line. One went squish and woosh, the other was silent. Now I had some direct feedback from the physical effort. A bicycle on the run is full of the sound of the wind; moving slowly, it takes on the sound of the road. Such association with a road and a cyclist must seem crazy to others. Yesterday I hardly spoke to anyone and some days I don't expect to talk to anyone. To me the road was like a make-believe person in the same way that children have imaginary friends. Children can have difficulties in relating to real people, I was having the same problem with the rational world. So many aspects of real life didn't make sense.

Day 7: Memories of home

I sit in a café in south Munich, so far away from home. Thoughts of home often come in the silliest of memories; English summers, green grass, coffee on the lawn and platefuls of lumpy chocolate cake. As long as I don't forget what I've left behind, there's a good chance I will return home.

Germany's chief city was the easiest one I'd crossed so far. In my mind I had a vision of the journey being but a series of scene changes. I thought of the Austrian Alps as being a theatrical backdrop, and the first snow-capped peak I saw looked as if it had been painted on glass.

Day 7: On the road to Innsbruck

I'm nervous, more apprehensive now as the journey leaves Germany. I promised myself that on reaching Austria I would be fit and strong enough to begin my race against time. If I become too complacent so early into the adventure, the lost time will be impossible to regain and I might as well pack my bags and go home.

The Bavarian Germany that discreetly interlocked with the foothills of Austria was beautiful. Sleepy-eyed cows gazed dreamily into space and their bells jangled in rhythm with their chewing of grass. Although I'd ridden through the most industrial part of Germany, I felt sorry to leave. There was a predictability about German people which made it safe. Certain characteristics here were similar to England which meant that I had some understanding of the way of life. The mechanical conservatism of such a life however, functioned better without the likes of me.

Slowly, I wound upwards towards Innsbruck, capital of the Tyrol, commanding the northern approach to the Brenner Pass. I imagined Austria to be somewhere north of Switzerland, but of course it was well east. My geography had room for improvement. Down the road descending to the valley of the river Inn, I plummeted. I was late for a meeting with my sponsors and so dashed across the gentle city as it leaned back in a concave of mountains. A girl on a moped directed me this way then that; she said through traffic and through lights; look straight ahead at the end of the main street, but I didn't, I looked left. In the valley of two tall town houses joined together by canopies and colour, there stood a scene that bewitched me. Market stalls supported the multi-coloured awnings, and the sweetest of fruit overflowed onto the street. Dressed in flimsy pinks and whites, boys and girls walked hand in hand. They were spotlit by the rapidly lowering sun, the image was fused with magic which nearly lasted a minute.

A small press conference had been arranged at my hotel in Innsbruck during which I drank two cups of coffee, four pints of orange juice, ate twelve sausage rolls, and three slabs of blackcurrant gateaux. I felt sick. In my hotel room I checked over my bike, cleaned my clothes and deposited the contents of my stomach into the lavatory. I felt better.

The people from Spar were very kind. As much as wishing to benefit commercially from the publicity of the adventure, I sensed they were equally intrigued by the nature of someone like me embarking on such a journey. Later that evening, having enjoyed half a carafe of wine with a steak, I wondered into the old town along Herzog Friedrich Strasse. The journey was taking shape. I was here to break a record. For a while this idea had lost its meaning. Fear of failure had pushed the record to the back of my mind. Eleven days into the adventure and I was not only on schedule but feeling fine. I felt more confident about the rest of the journey. My knee was no longer giving me any serious problems. As the Brenner Pass would be the first major mountain I would have to cross, this would be my first test.

A last minute flurry of rain lined the flat cobbles with a halo of street light that flushed along gutters and disappeared into drains.

Chocolate shops stood rich and clean where the most ornate chocolates in the world cost a week's wages. Halfway down the street a group of punks and drunks hung around. Restaurants closed their doors in turn, a mobile grill van dished out cheap chips. A drunk fell over; a punk threw up; someone urinated in the centre of the street. Innsbruck at night seemed to be cleansing itself of the excesses of the day.

Walking back to the hotel I thought about tomorrow's crossing into Italy. Northern Europe was to be replaced by a land renowned for its passion rather than its reason. My blood was beginning to stir and that was no bad thing.

At six o'clock in the morning it was cloudy, an hour later the sun dispersed overnight mist to reveal the promise of a warm day. Innsbruck was at the foot of the pass which rose 4,500 feet in 22 miles. Standing for a moment at the base, I enjoyed the anticipation of the beginning of the climb. My heart was thumping and I was breathing deeply. Whenever I climbed the side of a mountain I felt I was flying. Rising above the city so close and so quickly was the bicycle equivalent of vertical take off. Finding a rhythm almost immediately, my heartbeat slowed, my breathing became shallower and concentration narrowed on the most specific of observations. A column of ants marched in single-file from Austrian pine to European larch and its barrel-shaped, flat-ended brown cones. When the act of pedalling becomes automatic, the more receptive I become. I smelt the sweet scent of sawn wood and heard the far away crack of a tree being felled. One hairpin bend followed another as Austrian pines rattled their leaves. Half an hour passed without a pause and that became an hour. Any moment I expected to feel the onset of exhaustion, only then would I know if my fitness was of a sufficient calibre to resist the real duress that I knew was not too far away. Up and up into a pale blue sky, I felt the warm sun reddening my back.

The trickle of sweat that flowed down my back seemed to pour out of the tops of my shoulders. The rhythm was still intact and that would make me invulnerable to fatigue. When the rhythm cracks, each passing minute becomes an hour. An hour passed and I was no longer aware of anything except the road in front of me. I was no longer looking behind me, cared little for the cars that overtook me, and accepted now that the trees looked all the same. The wind was pushing me along, gusting occasionally and blowing the dust of the road around my wheels. Without the cooling effect of the wind against me, every part of my body vapourised into water. Looking down as I pedalled it was disquietening to see part of me dripping onto my shoes, onto my pedals and then onto the road. An hour turned into an hour and a half and I could feel the muscles in my legs beginning to pulsate. Just as a wounded finger might feel, throbbing with the heartbeat, so my legs, involuntarily, and with the subtlest of movement, swelled and tightened with every pedal turn. An hour and a half turned into two hours and rounding a corner the wind turned against me so I resolved to push even harder to the top. Quickly now I pressed on the pedals, but not once did I stand up and stamp. My form was good and my relief would only be crushed if I collapsed before the summit. After two and a half hours I at last saw an horizon and feeling distorted and feeble stood shivering overlooking the road to Bolzano, Italy and the magnificent limestone Dolomites.

In the Spring of '81 I rode round the edge of the Italian Alps, passing through Monte Carlo, the Riviera, and La Spezia. This time around, having crossed the lower Alps, I descended to Bolzano and Trento. So far I had ridden nearly 1,200 miles in eight days. If I'd driven a car at 30 miles per hour non-stop it would have still taken two days to get so far. The average distance covered each day was 150 miles, 20 miles a day down on schedule; 20 miles didn't seem so far, but over eight days it represented a full day's cycling. Until I was certain my knee had repaired sufficiently I had taken this slow build-up into account in my initial planning. Quietly I had told myself to remain calm and trust the advice of my surgeon and physiotherapist. 'As time heals,' they said, 'the knee will soon be strong.' The greatest strength I needed was the patience and confidence to be sure that time was right. I knew a balance had to be sought. If the world record was to be mine then I must simply cycle faster for longer; but if I cycled too fast for too long my knee would become inflamed and the journey around the world would end before Rome.

It was late afternoon when I reached the outskirts of Trento and as I cycled along looking for somewhere to eat, a lorry pulled up alongside and the driver lent out of his window and asked me in broken English, 'You wanna place to sleep, you follow me. Mia wife will make you the dinner, yes?'

With his large round cheeks and big laughing eyes he looked a cheery man and so I followed the lorry and before long sat chatting in the house of this thick-necked man who introduced himself as Luciano.

The room was sparsely furnished with one sideboard, three chairs, and a carpet the size of a doormat. 'So you are a cyclist? I too am a cyclist.' He looked the oddest shape for a cyclist that I'd ever seen. He started to roll up his trouser leg, presumably to show me the state of fitness of his calf muscles, but a barrel-shaped chest and very fat belly made it difficult for his short arms to reach. He slapped his thighs instead. 'Solid. I am very solid.' We chatted for an hour, me, on the edge of my chair, he, slapping his thighs. An hour passed, and a cup of tea later, his family still had not appeared. It occurred to me that something was possibly amiss. Here I was with a body as thin as an eel, a catch for a man the size of a whale. I became tense while the next half an hour passed. We continued to chat and while away the time. When he edged his chair a little closer I looked around for a way to escape. The doorbell rang. 'Mia wife, and the cheeldron,' and he smiled. The dinner table was set and we sat down and said grace.

I enjoyed watching Luciano eat. His teeth were hurting so he placed them in a glass on the sideboard. Such pearly choppers seemed a little lost outside his rather large head, but there was a reason; the pasta served the dual purpose of providing sustenance for himself, whilst at the same time, warming his aching gums. Fat round cheeks bulged in such a way as to process the maximum amount of pasta in the shortest space of time. With a face full of *fettuccine*, he talked.

'Mia wife, is she not beautiful, and the cheeldron, they are thee most beautiful bambinos no?' Horatio was cross-eyed and while looking his father in the eye, he booted me on the shin from under the table.

'Mia boy, I will giva hima the world.' Luciano looked down to eat, as I grimaced at the child, choking a little.

'Now we sleep,' said Luciano, turning to me, 'and mia wife will sleep there.' Looking at her, he pointed to the living room floor. My protestations fell on deaf ears, so with some reluctance, I laid out my sleeping bag on his double bed. He wasn't aware of my concern, and as it happened, that was the least of my problems. As his head faced towards God, his mouth fell open to reveal remnants of pasta wedged between brown teeth. He was like a sack of lard wrapped up in a string vest. Settling down to the back of his throat, his catarrah sent shock waves across the bed to me. Unable to sleep I watched the spiders steal across Luciano's dusty ceiling, they didn't stop moving until daybreak. As the sun rose I could barely keep my eyes open but said thank you and goodbye.

Day 9: From Trento to Florence via the road to Verona

All morning I cycled hard. I didn't speak, and no-one spoke to me for four hours. As I rode past cafés I drifted into and out of the sound of people. Cycling is a national sport in Italy and anyone with a little time to notice me, waves. Sitting on the bridge over the River Adige in Verona, I watched a column of ants trail their way. Several large red ones had the job of guarding a small black one, pushing it forward, guiding it in the direction they were going. I didn't know if they were protecting this little ant or whether it was on its way to be eaten. For a moment I felt like that small ant. I wondered if this journey would protect me or eventually eat me up.

In Verona, the main road from central Europe over the Brenner Pass intersects with the one that connects Venice to Milan.

Today the atmosphere was like treacle. On the road to Modena, the air stuck to every part of my body. The journey was taking shape; it went in straight lines. In between the tall trees, the long straight road rippled in the distance. As the heat of the day rose, haystacks bent and cow's legs bent as if made of rubber. The sun blazed, and the road was so hot, it dribbled into fields of flax. The road was punishing me again, and sometimes I wondered if it were my penance. Such days were never ending.

Modena wasn't very far from Bologna and then I had to cross over the Appennines to Florence. In the early evening light, the lower slopes of the Appennines were a maze of fences and stone walls which occasionally created the perfect square. It was a three-hour climb to the top, some twenty or so miles away. Getting steadily higher, I could feel this little mountain side taking hold of me, drawing me closer, demanding my attention to the fullest degree. This was not going to be an easy climb and I knew my concentration would be narrowed down to the act of my cycling up a mountain. The rhythm of this ascent was the most important part of today. Today was the most important day of the adventure, tomorrow was too far away and yesterday already past. Now I felt tired. I have been riding since 6 a.m. and at 7 p.m. the sun was already low over the horizon. In 13 hours I had cycled 170 miles. I reminded myself that today was *Day 9.* New cities I passed in the morning resembled those of the afternoon. Sharp and pristine before sunset, shadows that had followed me since sunrise, had similarly hardly changed.

Night began to fall and the moonlit shadows were lighter than those created by the setting sun. A nearly full moon was hiding behind a cloud which was scurrying as fast as it could. The night shift of dark clouds was due any moment. From where the moon was, it was she who crept from under each cloud. The road shone, universe-blue against black, and the shadow of my head looked laboured. This small pass over the Appennines would rise to 3,000 feet, the summit of which would take me four hours to reach. It was 9 p.m. and I was half-way. Fields that were once perfectly square turned to a more disorganised shambles. The mountain had taken on another guise. The trees' dark shadows flickered in a gentle breeze as I brushed past on my way to the summit. Once there, I would be half-way to Florence, and then it would all be downhill. As I bicycled in the silence and the darkness I became aware of the sound of my breathing as I have rarely been aware before. Maybe it was a combination of the effort and the nightime that was affecting my senses, but my breathing no longer felt part of me. It was as if the short gentle rasping of breath would have continued at the same rate had I been cycling or sleeping. My legs also, as if by their own voluntary accord, went round and round as if they were in control of their own actions within the body. The rhythm of the breathing complimented my rotating legs exactly and I felt my whole body had become a series of parts, each in tune with each other. Holding onto the tops of the handlebars I sat upright and breathed deeply, the crest of the summit could be seen in the moonlight and for a moment I was on the roof of the backbone of Italy.

I reached the summit and started the descent. I sped faster and my wheels glazed the road with the softest of footfalls. Between one bend and another I was like a plane, swooping and shifting, coming into land. In pitch darkness, it wasn't easy to judge the distance from the road to my wheel. I began to imagine I was flying. The white line was like the centre of a runway. The fireflies were landing flares. Descending, any moment now I would touch down. I could hear the occasional café with its bright lights and pinball machines in the distance. Clusters of paraffin lamps pin pricked the air in the same way a city is seen from the sky. The moon appeared bulbous and heavy. Mountains and cables and the very tops of the tallest trees gave the impression of having manacled her to the ground. Old women knitted by their lamps, as old men sat small children on their knee. Lusty farmhands chased the girls, as gangs of youths sloped along the walls, eyeing me with suspicion. I knew they would be more afraid of me than I of them. And with the moon as a backdrop, I continued to plunge, deep into the bowels of my second Italian night.

I crawled out of a hedge the following morning, and freewheeled the last mile into Florence. Finishing a *cappucchino* on the terrace of a small bar on the Piazza di San Firenze, I walked around the city centre to gather my early morning senses. An old tramp was slumped against the railings across the road. Pidgeons dropped their guava here and there. Saturday night and Sunday morning revellers filled the odd empty seat in the occasional deserted square. The dull house sparrow grated and chirped over sun-baked red rooftops. Sunday papers crinkled. Nearby, the famous *duomo*, one of the finest cathedrals built during the Renaissance, was a little tear-stained on its dark side. Further away, the church of Santa Croce wasn't yet open. It was so obviously fashionable for Florentine youths to walk in the vicinity of the *duomo*, in the centre of Florence. In a way, I envied the easy pattern of such enjoyment. This luxury of observing this beautiful city would prevent me completing today as planned. Tonight I had to be in Rome. It would take 14 hours to ride over 170 miles, and I would see very little of the surrounding countryside and nothing of the people. Travelling at such speed was tantamount to not travelling at all. After Sienna, less than two hours south of Florence, I would lunch on the slopes of Mont Amiata. I might have a quick paddle in Lake di Bolsena, dinner in Viterbo and sometime before midnight, a snatched sleep in the chaos of Rome. Instead of having to fight through the snarled Roman traffic, a long bottleneck jam had made my cycling across the centre a good deal easier. This was fortunate as after such a hard day I was now on the verge of exhaustion. The congestion was caused by a smashed motorbike beside which was the impression of a body completely covered in a white sheet. A pool of blood lay beside the bike. My exhaustion seemed a small price to pay in comparison. As I checked into the Cavalieri Hilton all I could think of before falling sound asleep was, so much for *Day 10*.

Day 11: Breakfast in the Cavalieri Hilton

This morning's breakfast consists of: one mango, two papayas, four mangosteens, two bowls of corn flakes, a small bowl of porridge, a portion of eggs and bacon, a glass of orange juice, a croissant, and three cups of black coffee. Slightly more varied than my usual morning meal of jam and bread dunked into a litre of milk.

Several Press committments in Rome left me a little behind schedule, and I didn't reach Naples when expected. The first flight of the journey was from Tel Aviv to Athens and then to Bombay. It was only 12 days away, but cycling almost hour to hour, it seemed an eternity. Fifty miles north of my intended overnight stop I ate quickly in a bar and searched out a quiet field well away from the main road. A group of youths on motorbikes passed me twice, but when no one was around, I stole into the heart of an orchard in darkness. The air was humid and any thought of sleep was prevented by images which raced inside my head. The day, the miles, cities and faces, thoughts of home and distant lands all jumbled together and looked the same.

Mosquitos bit my face and arms as I tried to clear my sleeping space of rocks. Whilst designed to harden me for what was to come, this part of the journey had completed the training. Both mind and body had to be hard and strong, there was no room for weakness now.

I heard the noise of a train approaching. A slight breeze caught the leaves of a hedgerow behind me, and a few leaves scattered. The sound of the train was louder. Beneath me, the ground trembled. Then it shook, and the noise was a roar. The train was coming straight for me and before I could move, the filthy black outline of a sparking freight train thundered and screamed as I involuntarily covered my ears with my hands. A minute passed, maybe two as heavy rolling stock creaked and whined and the sound of tearing metal was all around me. In the dark, I had camped an arm's length away from the busiest railway line in Southern Italy. I laughed out aloud, I felt a little mad. I moved to the centre of the field. As the evening stillness reasserted itself, the sound of motorbikes replaced the train. A gang of youths touted burning torches as they parked alongside my field. They looked towards me and I froze. I knew they couldn't see me. Surely they couldn't see me? When they climbed off their bikes, I prepared to flee. Into the field they peered, the glow of their torches was perilously close. If they saw me I would be an excellent evening's entertainment. I could be their hare, racing around in circles until they worried me to death. The firelight made mean faces hideous. Whatever they were going to do, it would be soon. Had the café told the local gang somebody new was in town? Walking around in circles, they remained safely on the outskirts of this very dark field. With a hysterical cry, they plied the torches to tinder-dry gorse and in an instant the field was encircled in flames. They waited and laughed, the prey was as quiet as a mouse, only the eyes darted to and fro. The fire spread and still they waited. I could smell the smoke, any moment I would cough and they'd be onto me like a ferret to a rabbit. On the outskirts of a town, this was as much a jungle as anywhere I'd been. In a mocking gesture, the four youths stood, and under my breath I cursed them. The bastards. Residents of nearby houses shouted the alarm and that was their signal to leave. Kick-starting their bikes they laughed and cried out, shouting inanely into the night. Calmly collecting my few possessions, I found a gap in the hedgerow that hadn't caught fire. Where I lay earlier was already alight.

Looking back a moment later, I saw the hedgerow on fire. Half a mile further down the railway track, I could see the orchard in flames, surrounded by two vehicles with flashing blue lights. I laid out my sleeping bag and stared open-eyed at the rest of the universe. If anyone was watching us, I hoped they understood the unprovoked, unreasoning hatred of these boys for a stranger who wished them no harm. I didn't. With difficulty I forced myself to sleep.

The following morning I rode into the dawn, dishevelled, with straw matted in my hair. Last night's field was charred and smoking.

Naples was a colossal mess. For thirty miles I laboured into and out of the city through narrow cobble streets. Traffic was at a standstill, and it looked as if it had been there a week. Horns sounded and tempers flared as lunchtime came and went. Tall town houses faced each other menacingly, ideal for street fights, protected as they were by their height. On the slopes of Vesuvius by the gates of Pompeii, you didn't need to be astute to see that life was a struggle. Naples didn't have the immediate grandeur of Florence or the sophistication of Rome, but it had its own charm. Filtering through the city sounds I heard a young boy play his trumpet from a balcony above. Listening to his gentle serenade gave me a warm feeling. As the waiting became interminable, pure notes slipped into spaces not even a bicycle could attempt to squeeze through. As I moved slowly forward the tune of the trumpet player receded, and within the scramble of people and places I marvelled at this, the sweetest of sounds.

The Tyrrhenian coast of Italy had the lack of finesse of Blackpool or Miami. Such resorts catered for the masses in the same way: the beaches were crammed with overtired children and overweight sunbathers, both cooked to a crisp. An army of deckchairs held onto all the commanding positions; several positioned in a circle, marked out the territory of a family having a good time. This part of Italy I didn't like. I made a mental note for all the people who said this journey would be the experience of a lifetime; that I would meet interesting people, that I would have time to think about my life, that only far away places could provide me with such adventure. They were wrong. The human race can be foolish, sensuous, crazy, loving, charming, hateful, dead or alive anywhere in the world, at any given time. Next summer, I resolved to sip English tea on the Blackpool Prom, and watch the people go by.

After riding through Salerno, I turned left at Battapaglia and headed inland towards Potenza. It was ages since I'd thought about the world record, but all of a sudden it dominated any thoughts in my mind. Today was *Day 12*, and I had cycled nearly 2000 miles. To give in to serious fatigue at this stage would jeopordise the journey. I did ache, and it was hard, but to bleed in the joints and weep by the side of the road was a humiliation I hadn't yet endured. In sunny golden fields, rolls of straw stood to attention; farmers stood by water sprinklers which sprayed me and the long straight road.

As I began to climb the lower slopes of Mount Cervialto on the way to the lands of Lucania, my body reached a state of physical and mental equilibrium. The amount of energy I used would be in proportion to the energy and rest ingested. Having spent so much time riding alone, away from people, I no longer felt threatened by their absence. Lined by Lombardy poplar trees, the road twisted and turned, and for the first time during the journey I felt happy. At this moment, as the shadows began to get longer, I was simply cycling around the back woods of Italy. Watching the farmer tend his crops made me feel at ease. It was the trees that decided where I should go. Continuing the climb, I noticed that whenever my fatigue started to overcome me, the trees became closer together and the fields were hidden. The more tired I became, the more the tall trees engulfed me, and everyday life on either side of the road

would be lost. The trees were all around me. They were guiding me, shielding me, concentrating my vision on a tunnel that was the route around the world. Today, I was on my bike for 16 hours.

After the six-mile climb out of Vietri di Potenza I started to look for somewhere to sleep. Over the years of travelling I've developed a system of sleeping safely outdoors which is almost foolproof. In the middle of the uninhabited Nubian Desert, the system is quite flexible – I sleep wherever I collapse at the end of the day. Without people to bother me, the procedure is fairly simple. With people milling curiously about, it becomes more complicated and I am careful to the point of paranoia. I always try to cycle into a village just as night falls. In Africa, villages don't usually have street lights and the darkness is total. Before settling down to a meal in full view of everyone, I used to ride out of town in the direction I intended to take the following morning. Trying not to look conspicuous, which was not easy since I was probably the only white man in several hundred square miles, I cast a glance over any suitable wide-open field. Most people are afraid to go out at night, so away from the confines of the village I would be fairly safe. Having found a suitable spot, I would return to the village to eat, leaving when finished, and ride coolly away to my field. Anyone who thought of doing me harm would almost certainly not follow me, and those who did, would have to fall over me first. This system is only 'almost foolproof' however. Once, completely lost in Uganda, I slept out on the shores of Lake Albert. There was no-one around, but coming towards me I heard the sound of thundering hooves. Within an instant I was surrounded by twenty or more hippos galumphing along to their cool evening grazing lands. They didn't know I was there and wouldn't have bothered about me if they did. Treading on a cyclist is of no great consequence to a hippopotamus.

Fortunately, this was unlikely to happen in Southern Italy. On the top of a hillside overlooking the walled town of Peratin, I munched an enormous ham sandwich and drank a litre of milk. From every nook and cranny in the blackness of the valley, a dog barked. In the city centre a cathedral, lit like a grotto, glowed in the distance.

I slept fitfully with the wind blowing in my hair and I was glad to ride into and out of Potenza. After bearing south-east to Grassano the autostrada headed towards Altamura. Tiny holes of light pulled me through long dark tunnels as the road swept under my wheels. Hidden away in yellow neon light, it felt as if I was stationary and the rest of the world was moving. Tunnels turned into viaducts which amplified the sound of trains. Cicadas in their thousands chattered as would a steam-engine chugging up hill. Hour after hour I pedalled towards Taranto, on the way to Brindisi and the tail-end of Italy.

I was looking forward to leaving Italy because that meant I had nearly conquered Europe. It was nearly time to enter unknown lands, a world of fantasy and imagination. There was only Greece between me and Asia Minor, a simple matter of four days' cycling.

On the west side of Taranto, red-brick warehouse walls flaked into a sludge-coloured sea. Cranes rose like pinnacles, encircled by grubby clouds. Tethered so as to hide the sun, seedy-undergrowth docklife flourished and followed me through every slimy back alley. Sleazy youths on mopeds sidled

up to me, teasing me unashamedly. A cyclist on the road is tasty meat for 'banditos'. I asked a policeman the way to Brindisi. He whistled to five of his pals and they escorted me whining and roaring through the traffic and red lights.

Three hours later, I was in Brindisi. I bought my ticket, £17 for my passage to Greece, after which I had to rush through the formalities. Another agency gave me my boarding pass which police emigration duly stamped. Spending my leftover lire, I loaded my bike with bread, milk, a bar of chocolate and a bag full of raisins. For the first time in the journey it was like being on holiday. I felt so happy and my spirit was as free as a bird. As I laid out my sleeping bag on my own little piece of deck, the sun set, the horn hooted, and we drifted and whooshed and sailed out to sea.

Day 14: Starting to leave Europe behind

Normally it takes about three weeks for me to acclimatise to a journey, this time I have to adjust to the rhythm of the adventure straightaway. The more I think of Dad, of home, of friends; the harder the journey becomes. I have to totally disassociate myself from everything I know. At last, the journey is beginning to develop an identity which allows me to focus more directly on the task in hand. At this very moment, sitting on a white wall on the outskirts of Igoumenitsa, the sun shining, the sky a pretty deep blue, there is nothing else I think I want or need.

I could never say Igoumenitsa properly. Igmenouistos sounded similar, but no-one seemed to know of its existence. I knew the feeling. Every moving day eroded the differences between one city and the next, each city began to resemble all cities. Igoumenitsa had white walls upon which hung cheerful sprays of bright red bougainvillea. But then, every town and village I passed through owned such walls and such adornments. On my map, there were several routes to the villages; you could meander up gullies awash with mountain streams; donkey ride alongside ridges and peaks, dripping with cloud; or you could fly over the streams and the peaks, high above the clouds. On a bicycle there was only one practical route – the long straight road. Punishing those who dared tread its weary way, it also comforted, cajoled and caressed in times of need. It showed me the way to wherever I thought I wanted to go. It also tied me up in a straight line.

As I climbed out of Igoumenitsa, a thick green object lay near the middle of the road. It was a snake, and judging by its thickness, quite poisonous. Edging around at a distance I saw no sign of life, and placing my bike on the roadside, stepped a little closer. The road was silent, save for yellow butterflies scraping the air. Still the snake didn't move. Still I edged closer. Hot air rose undisturbed from the surface of the road, and roadside shrubs were quite still. I had an unreasoning fear of snakes not having seen too many, but peering from within smelling distance, it was obvious the poor thing was dead. They say the skin of a snake is dry, that they're blind and really rather timid. Leaning over its large green body, ever so slowly I touched the scrawny limp creature. It hissed. My God! It was alive. It moved, I jumped, it lunged. I didn't know what to do. It snapped, I leaped for my bike and as it slithered painfully toward me, I pedalled like the wind, hardly pausing to breathe.

The last snake I had seen slithered under my front wheel on a lonely road in Sri Lanka. I rode over the tip of its tail, and retaliating, it missed my ankle by a whisker. I had hoped to see more wildlife, but sightings were more myth than reality. In Africa I saw hippos and ostriches, crocodiles in the Nile; elephants climbed ridges with the nimbleness of antelopes; in the Nubian, a peregrine falcon circled above. I never saw a snow leopard in Nepal.

Day 15: The indulgence of being alone

It's been days now since I last spoke at length to anyone and I am becoming trapped by my own thoughts. Unlike the round-the-world sailors, I do see people and am not totally alone. But when I meet a kindly wrinkled old peasant, how well can we really communicate? The sailor can sit in his cabin and drift with the wind, he can read, write, talk on the radio and think. Cycling 170 miles every day, I have trouble simply thinking.

Pausing to take a photograph I saw a wrinkled old peasant creep out from behind a rock. Walking towards me he held out his hand, which I shook. He grasped my palm gently and without letting go stared into my face. Aware now of his calloused hands eating into my own, I started to ease my way out of his grip. His hand stretched around mine to create a bottle-neck between fingers and thumb. I likewise returned my grip to make a firm response. His hold packed tight my hand and his knuckles whitened. Ever so slowly I began to squeeze, and almost imperceptibly his expression became more playful. Having smiled the broadest of smiles revealing his only remaining tooth, he looked for a gesture that indicated it was still a game. I smiled back. He tightened his grip. His hands were strong, but my grip was younger. My teeth clenched as our hands locked. His eyes twinkled as we played our game but his smile was now taut and the veins in his neck throbbed. Each new meeting on the journey was a test. The old man loosened his grip and smiled. Fishing in his pocket he gave me a bundle of cheese. Searching in my pannier I pulled out my diary and made the motion to him to sign his name and so validate this section of today's ride. Without a word he took hold of my precious book, made a gesture of thanks and walked away. 'It's not a present,' I shouted, beginning to run after him, 'you can have something else if you like.' He wasn't running, scampering playfully more like in between the rocks. 'I'd like my book back now thank you,' I said, forgetting that he didn't understand me. He smiled and pausing, beckoned me to him, and then carried on, jockeying from one boulder to the next. I clambered over a large boulder and slid down a small slope of burning scree banging my knee so it bled. 'You half-brained peasant,' I shouted, 'give me my goddamn book.' I was furious. He began to laugh, but it was the strangest sound, like the whinnying of a goat and when he followed me down to the bottom of the slope and crouched next to me, his nostrils were flared. As I reached out for my diary he snatched it away again until I was breathing in his breath which smelt of dung. I stood up and we faced each other. He smiled in the same way a dog smiles with distemper, his skin was maggoty. He touched me on the shoulder and his eyes were red and leered. Glancing in the distance, past his head, my eyes diverted his attention and in that instant I jerked the book from his hand. I stepped back immediately and the arm that had rested on my shoulder fell to his side. I smiled, this old lame goat only wanted to play, but the game was over.

It was such a hot Greek summer's day. Today I would be climbing until evening and so gently I planned out a small strategy; 30 minutes rest every 3 hours. The sun bore down beautifully, the wind blew me east and I was strong. I was also determined to forge ahead and try and instil within me some notion of urgency. As mid-morning approached I stopped at a small roadside teashop.

'Come and sit down, let me buy you a coke.' A young family sitting around one of the tables beckoned me to join them. The older man spoke to me, 'you are English, yes? I can tell. Where do you think we come from?'

'Yugoslavia,' I guessed, knowing the border was not too far away.

'Good try. Czechoslovakia. At absurd rates of foriegn exchange, we are on holiday.'

For a moment I felt embarrassed. In all my travels I had never met anyone from an Eastern-bloc country and I felt privileged. They were very friendly and whilst being polite, retained a bearing that was both dignified and restrained. 'How we should like to travel more, but we both saved four months' salary to live on Corfu these past three and a half weeks. Now we have squeaky brakes and must drive home slowly.' They looked thoughtful. They had been a little bothered by the numbers of Britons holidaying on Corfu, 'the frequency of their drinking was great,' they said, a little uncomprehending, and they asked me if it was an English tradition to take off your clothes in public places? We chatted, and without intruding, he asked, 'what are you doing?'

'Cycling around Greece,' I said.

He became thoughtful again, refraining from making the obvious remarks.

'Ah yes. It must be amusing to do as you do. This is not possible for us. We are allowed our holidays and then we must return to work,' and he sighed. Such a way of life didn't seem very different from that of the West. 'But with no disrespect, when the factories have to be manned and the fields have to be cut, I do wonder why you embark on such an odyssey?' he continued with a curiosity which I found rather unnerving.

For those few seconds, this man had made me unsure about my journey. I felt a little frivolous. We shook hands goodbye and as I freewheeled down the otherside of the hill, the Czech and his wife passed me with their squeaky brakes and threw me a couple of hard-boiled sweets.

Following the river Kalamas towards Ioannina, between sun-bleached rocks and scattered patchy scrub, I climbed and descended until early afternoon. I was completely alone now, and pushing hard on the pedals I forced round a rhythm, up, up, up to the top and then down. Climbing so many hills, I came to the conclusion that the creation of a rhythm has several different parts; relaxing into a gentle receptive state of mind slightly precedes an awareness of time which in turn preceeds the point where time becomes meaningless. Time for me, was the completion of one rotation of the pedal which replicates itself nearly exactly, hundreds of times up every mountain. In such a way the course of a day passed. Without such fluidity of motion, too much energy would be expended to finish a day's ride. Although being aware of each rotation of the pedal at the bottom of the mountain, I quickly became oblivious not only to the pedal movement but to time passing. My senses had been over-exposed to the pedalling, and in a

similar way, so had my view of the long straight road after spending over 14 hours staring at whatever road stretched out before me. Occasionally something new would sparkle my dull rhythm, a snake in the road or a peasant creeping from behind a rock. The road swerved away from the river and I emptied my water-bottle. This mountainside was longer than I had expected, half-way to the summit the wind began to drop and the sweat dribbled out of every pore. I tried to think of a happy thought but it wasn't easy. With eyes stinging, I edged my way towards the crest of a hill.

Eventually I reached the small town of Ioannina and on the shores of a green lake lunched on bread and cheese. Blue sky was quickly turning grey as a flurry of rain scattered still waters. The locals said there was a mountain to climb, the Metsovan Pass, and it was so long, I wouldn't reach the top until evening.

It was raining as I rode slowly up the lower slopes of the Mitsikeli Range. The wind was buffeting from behind and to my right, the Lake of Ioannina began to appear far away. Ferns flapped from here to the lake shore, and it was they which robably accounted for the green waters. Grey clouds now began to blacken and the rain began to pour. Landing on my bare legs, large voluptuous raindrops splashed. I continued to climb, hoping to cover as much ground as possible before having to shelter. In the distance, the lake, still green, was small. The wind pushed me forward as I slowly began to enter into a rhythm. All my energies, physical and emotional, had to be isolated into performing one action only, reaching the top of this pass. Climbing a mountain provided the peace of mind and well-being that comes from establishing a rhythm. Every climber seems to feel the same way. Every ordinary person going out for a regular run usually returns with some sublime feeling. However, the rain caused not only my lovely green lake to disappear, but for a time, absolutely everything else. The rain teemed as I wound up the longest mountain climb of the adventure so far. Lorries passed in a frenzy of spray and blaring horns, I simply passed in a frenzy. Two hours passed then three, and in the wind and pounding rain my mind was a whirl of colours. Four hours after beginning this climb, the mountain had made me delirious and I no longer felt I was riding a bicycle. I was riding a bird, I was a bird soaring, flapping. My judgement of today was impaired in exactly the same way as when I climbed the Appennines. Neither then nor now could I differentiate between what was real and what was not. The one common factor was climbing a mountain. The rhythm was everything. It was like a Tibetan chant ringing every movement of my body into an even pace. It was a mantra, just as if I were sitting in a quiet room with my eyes gently closed. On the far side of the valley, the mountains and the mists were one, and as the rain trickled down what looked like a canvas, landforms that had been there since time immemorial had the uniformity of runny paint. The rain was a torrent and there was nowhere to hide. Looking at mountain-top pinnacles half-toned by the intervening wash, I asked myself yet again, what it was all about. I remembered a poem from my childhood:

Child, do not go
Into the dark places of the soul
For there the grey wolves whine,
The lean grey wolves.

Another hour passed and quickly now I forced the pace. Never before, on the journey so far, had I been acquainted with such feelings. Slowly riding over the crest of the mountain, I decided, on account of the rapidly failing light, to commence the descent immediately. For the first ten miles I plummeted, for the second ten miles it was pretty fast, the last ten miles were marginally less frantic.

Arriving at the campsite in Meteora at 10 p.m., I was buzzing and knew I wouldn't sleep for at least another couple of hours. The reception desk was occupied by an English girl on a work exchange programme, and she introduced herself as Coraline. After I'd showered and washed my rain-soaked clothes, she asked me to join her for supper. Positioned as she was, between a bottle of ouzo and a plate of dried fish and moussaka, Coraline had one of those deadpan expressions which made it difficult to gauge her feelings. At first she didn't speak, just sniggered at everything I said. I became aware that she was also sniggering at herself sniggering and it was difficult to say which came first. 'I've got lice,' she said quite by surprise, groping about in a mass of unruly hair. I began to realise why she had asked me, so suddenly, to eat with her; no one else would. I liked her. Swallowing hard on the moussaka, she said, 'I'm alien you know. I don't fit in here.' There was a pause. 'Come to think about it, I don't seem to fit in anywhere.'

'I understand only too well the world you live in, I've been there myself.'

'Its better there,' she shrugged, 'better the fear of the little known than the tragedy of the familiar.' After shaking her hair vigorously, she slugged back another ouzo. Placing my hand above her knee, she looked at me intently. 'Feel those thighs,' she invited me, 'I

reckon I could cycle around the world.'
She laughed, 'if I was stupid enough to
do so.'

'Better be stupid and cycle around
the world than be just plain stupid,' I
replied peevishly. Her remark had
angered me, not because she might be
right, simply that she had nothing better to offer. For a while we sat in
silence.

'It's all to do with sad muscles in the
face,' she explained softly, 'too much
melancholy and the muscles become
sad.' Smiling, she continued, 'sad faces
are a bit like happy toes, they both indicate times past and times present. How
often the wonder of a first meeting
quickly turns to disappointment. Toes
on the other hand, do not usually have
a great deal to do with first encounters.'
Looking away from me, she carried on
talking, not to anyone in particular. 'If
only people would talk to toes, their
miserableness could be covered up with
their socks.'

The following morning I left Meteora
and breakfasted at a garage near Lárisa.
Six men sat around a small white table
drinking red wine and they asked me to
join them. All had big hands, with large
gold wedding rings squeezing red flesh
around short fat fingers. Engrained
with wrinkles and soil, each face was
decorated with a broad moustache,
unshaven chin, long-haired eyebrows
and long swept-back jet-black hair.

'Hey Ingleesh, where you go, Theo?'

Thessaloníki was my next stop and
after I nodded yes, I drew a circle in the
air. It was supposed to represent cycling around the world, but it could have
meant riding to Theo and back, it
didn't matter. A young boy brought me
a plate of sliced tomatoes in vinaigrette
dressing only to present to the table a
bunch of freshly pulled sprouts.

'You see these,' one of the men said,
shaking several bugs from the inside of
the bunch, 'they no good. In fact, they
are very, very bad,' and he laughingly
pointed his finger at me. A discussion
continued about the number of bugs
falling off when shaken, and not being a
bug expert I decided to stick at what I
knew best and headed off towards
Theo.

As the wide floodplains of Thessalía
opened up, the river Piniós meandered
alongside the road. After Lárisa I
turned north towards Platamon and
Kateríni and by evening reached the
outskirts of Thessaloníki. After a poor
night's sleep I bore east again to
Asprovalta and Kavalla, stopping in a
small village called Paradisos, ten miles
short of Xánithi. As I freewheeled onto
a pavement stacked with old men and
straight-backed sit-up wooden chairs, I
was tense with urgency. It was hard to
know exactly the distance covered
today, but it approached at least 160
miles. These past two days I had hardly
spoken a word and now I was conscious
only of a need to reach the Middle East.
Turkey was a day away and the Syrian
border four to five days ride. Having
bathed in the icy-cold waters of the village fountain, I sat down in a café and
ordered half a roasted chicken. A
moment of paranoia flashed before me;
what if the Jordanian authorities refuse
me entry on the grounds that I would be
continuing my journey through Israel?
Overland entry into such disputed territory is allowed but is rare. In the planning of this part of the journey I tried to
take into consideration every eventual-
ity. Each day's distance had been carefully worked out, my visas were in
order, airports were presently open, I
carried nothing in my bags, like
weapons, that would otherwise restrict
my entry. Surely nothing could go

wrong? As I pondered and cycled the last few miles of the day, I began to think of the evening meal. Everyday I promised myself a hot dinner, something to look forward to, and the sizzling hot chicken that I so much wanted tonight was not very far away.

On both sides of the narrow road, old men lined up for their evening game of dominoes. Four cafés stood opposite each other and I knew this would be the last time before crossing into Turkey that I could fill my nostrils with Greek aromas. My tomato salad was red as blood and the onions were as sharp as they were cutting. The chicken was succulent, and with wedges of freshly baked bread, I mopped up all the juice. A guitar sounded amidst the chatter and the clacking of thrown dice and as it grew dark, antique street lamps slowly glowed white. Lamplight streaked along telephone wires as a young man proudly showed off his new born son.

'Hey you wanna see my new baby?' he asked me, holding a sweet smelling bundle. 'It's beautiful,' I said, but it had a rather large head and a very flat face. This baby was solid and would one day have a thick neck. Pleased with my admiration, the father sauntered across the road to talk to an old man. 'They thought I was not a real man because my wife have no baby, but now I show them...'

A young fellow behind me sniggers. 'He is a proud man, this man, but when baby grow up, it will look like the eighteen year old butcher's boy who delivers meat to his wife every day.'

Suddenly, in a flurry of speed, a car dashed through that quiet little street and knocked down a mottled-black cat. The cat squirmed and twitched, and her tiny chest heaved in a spasm. Blood trickled in gentle spurts from a pretty freckled mouth until a pool formed to red-stain her face. Her head did not move but the back did. Contorted and strained the cat fell. An old man dragged it to the kerb. I closed my eyes for a moment, wishing it hadn't happened. After another cup of coffee I decided to leave and look for a nice hedge to sleep by. As I mounted my bike I saw a couple of mottled-black kittens sitting patiently under my chair. Mum said she was just nipping out for a few bits for tea. She said she'd only be a couple of minutes.

The following morning I rode over the River Maritza, this particular bridging point was manned by guards of Greece and Turkey. I passed into Turkey and at long last left Europe behind. Waiting in the queue to pass through immigration, an English fellow called me over to his lorry.

'Your English aren't you? Here, have something to eat,' and he passed me a half-opened can of stewed steak. 'I'm an Astran lorry driver, I do the round trip to Baghdad eight times a year.' They were a rough breed, drivers who ventured so far, but they were honest with their own kind. We ate in silence as the sun began to set. He could be here for days until the customs certified his right of entry. After a tin of cold rice pudding, washed down with a mug of steaming hot tea, I said goodbye and carried on my separate way.

Riding into the end of a day, I heard the echo of a barking dog in the distance. Small children in dirty torn shirts ran after me, asking for cigarettes. Sounding their horns, more Astran drivers passed me as gently as they could, they understood how hard it was. Pedalling faster and faster into a darkening sky, another day had almost gone. As the night plunged me into darkness the colour of pitch, there was at least some consistency in the journey and I was strangely reassured. Alone and faraway, somewhere in the middle of nowhere, I unpacked my sleeping bag, climbed inside, and closed my eyes.

4 · THE MIDDLE EAST

I was going to have to cross Turkey very quickly to keep anywhere near to my Middle East schedule. I had ridden until the early hours of the morning, so I should reach the outskirts of Istanbul well before lunchtime. It was with such regret that I didn't stop for a long in the city that sits astride the Bosporus, filled with the grimy, pungent market smells of unkempt Asia. The adventure would now require more than its fair share of luck. Feeling a strong wind blow from the west, I breathed a sigh of relief. For three days the wind blew me forward, at first east, then south-east. During the day, I didn't stop cycling for more time than it took to eat and drink. At night I snatched four hours sleep on the side of the road. For three days I was beyond caring. The mountains rose and fell and I, like an ant, hung onto the steepest of rises, surfacing again and again over the crest of yet another mountain. Plodding along at 12 miles per hour, 20 hours cycling would give me the necessary mileage to enter Syria on time. I had seriously underestimated the distance across Turkey and if it hadn't been for my fifteen years of cycling experience, this adventure would have ground to a halt somewhere between Ankara and Kayseri. For three days I saw nothing but sun-bleached outcrops of God forsaken rock sur-rounded by the beginnings of a wilderness. Unlike the climb over the Metsovan Pass, or the imminent ride over the edge of the Syrian desert, Turkey presented me with not a single disturbing physical feature. Instead it wore me down with a mechanical consistency that was worthy of any hard corner of the world. I didn't speak for two days and, for the rest of my time on that unforgiving road, heard only the sound of passing cars.

Day 20 started 60 miles north of Adana, and with the wind still blowing in my favour, I whisked through Seyban and landed in a dusty heap by a kebab salon on the outskirts of Antakya. Catching sight of myself in a mirror, my white eyes peeped out of a tired face which was lightly dusted in clay. The owner of the salon had a large German Kaiser moustache which twitched everytime he spoke.

'Perhaps young sir would like a kebab?,' he said in remarkable English. At this time of the day there was a distinct possibility his cupboard would be bare, so I said yes but asked only for tomato salad to follow. 'I could think of nothing that would delight me more,' and with a shifting glance to the kitchen, he temporarily disappeared. This, I decided, was no ordinary café proprietor. On the rather world-stained

white-washed wall, a poster hung, showing a bleached black and white photograph of a man with a twitching moustache. In large black lettering, the poster advertised the next performance of *The Great Mercutio*.

'Yes, it is I,' said the salon owner bringing me my daintily fried kebab. 'You are a suprised young man, I know these things. My father was a juggler, but I, well, I speak to the people.'

Sweat-stained and exhausted, I was incredulous. A man with a twitching moustache on the very edge of Turkey, began to recite Shakespeare:

Age cannot wither her nor her customs stale

Her infinite variety and her other women cloy

Their, um, appetites even though she makes them 'er

Hungry and then she makes them very satisfied.

The 'er vilest things have 'er become themselves and

in her the holy priests bless her um for 'er her...

'Oh, what is that blasted word?' and he cursed again.

'Stamina?' I said.

'Yes, of course, stamina,' and he clapped his hands.

'Make a bow,' I said.

'Of course,' he said and he craned his

body almost to the floor. I applauded and in my own withered state, over-compensated with perhaps too much gusto.

'Nay, young sir, please, such rapture, it is not a performance for all, it is only for you.' The Great Mercutio would not hear of payment for the meal, he said the exchange of a few worldly thoughts was payment enough.

'Syria, you will find that way,' he said nodding to his right, and after he shook my hand, I stepped onto the street, out of one dream and into another.

As the sun set, water sprinklers stopped sprinkling and groups of village women stopped tending the crops. Heaving clumsy hoes wearily on their backs, they waved as I passed. Before long I reached the perimeter fence which separated Syria from Turkey, and at intervals, look-out turrets manned with boy-soldiers watched my progress. For whatever reason, there is always tension at borders. On entering Syria, I would technically be in the Middle East, and I could only imagine what adventure would befall me there. A hiss of air came from my front tyre and the wheel rim bounced on the road. Of all the stupid places to puncture! As I climbed off the bike to repair the hole, a glint of field glasses gave me the feeling my every movement was being observed. This could mean trouble. Voices from a turret shouted, presumably telling me not to stop, and when I obviously carried on with what I was doing, half a dozen youths in combat uniforms ran towards me, brandishing short-grip Uzi machine guns. Border guards are notoriously unpredictable, some are good, others less so, and in that moment a journey through Uganda flashed before me. Cycling to Kampala during my journey to the source of the

Nile, I was held at gunpoint in the jungle late at night. The commanding officer demanded he ride my bike to which I naturally agreed. As he over-balanced, the first attempt it could be said, was unsuccessful. So far it was good fun. Falling off a second time was a disaster, and even funnier. The third time he rode into a tree. I had a fore-boding. He turned to me and threatened to chop me up with his machete if I didn't leave that instant. He stared at me from very close quarters as I looked into his eyes, seething with contempt. I could feel his hatred and tried to understand his hurt. I was scared. I imagined him dismembering my limbs, shooting off my arms to feed them to pigs that munched old turnips in the middle of the road. He wanted to machine-gun my thoughts so that they coloured the ground grey. Mucus and blood would splatter my cycling jersey. I remember thinking the oddest thought, that having washed the jersey clean that very day, I need not have bothered. As well as being very scared, I was also very excited. The adrenalin pumped through my body as I pedalled away like the wind. Now I am a little older and more experienced in these matters. I am still afraid.

Hearing panting breath, the guards were close now. Who was to say this situation would be any different? That they wouldn't exploit an innocent situation for their own gain and amusement. Expecting to be jostled immediately on my way, I proffered my passport to show that I meant no harm. They were stern folks these young boys with their guns and, depending on whether they were late for their tea, they would either let me go or detain me overnight. Instead, and to my suprise, they insisted, probably out of sheer bore-dom, on repairing my puncture. Set-

41

ting about the task with great endeavour, they tried this way then that to take off the tyre. Again and again they trapped the innertube, several times repairing the holes they'd created. One of the boys trapped a thumb, another spilt glue down the barrel of his gun and the others, helpless with laughter, advised in some depth as to their method of mending a front wheel. Short and cocky, one young man intimated the bicycle pump could be played with in an entirely different fashion. I grabbed hold of it and put it back on the bike, out of harm's way. It was like a scene from the Keystone Cops but in Turkish. When eventually I suggested leaving, each of the guards wanted to shake hands with me. Having done that once, they insisted on doing it again. It was getting dark so I told them that if we carried on shaking hands like this I'd end up staying the night. They seemed to like that idea so I extricated myself rather quickly and pedalled smartly through the formalities of the border.

Between Turkey and Syria, there is a five-mile stretch of no man's land where the blackest of nights and the most piercing of stars possess a country all of their own. Climbing steadily, my front tyre slowly began to deflate, and each time I pumped it up I was only able to ride a few hundred yards. It was too dark to do anything else, and if I wasn't careful, the Syrian border would close and complications might then occur. It was harsh of me to say, but the Turkish guards had not excelled themselves. As I wound up through unknown territory the air was spooky and surely I heard the strains of a flute in the wind? Around the bend of a hill it became louder, a little further on it became clearer and tucked away in a

nest of strangled trees, there stood the source of the music. A circle of stone columns rose to face a rising full moon. Standing alone by these towering Corinthian pillars, I was transported to the days of great armies on the march. Columns of men camped in the grounds of temples of the gods, and the moon rose for them in much the same way it did for me now. Why should I leave, no one would find me? Here I was in a secret land of my own where for one night I could be god of the moon, and as the wind whistled through the columns, I could pretend to conduct an orchestra of flutes. I so wanted to rest, and sitting for a minute in such awe-inspiring shadows, imagine myself to be anywhere but here, then I could come back, and enjoy the discovery all over again. Instead, I pumped up my tyre and leaving the deepening siren of the temple, wound my way towards the dim flourescence of the Syrian customs post.

Syrian customs were a shambles. From what sounded unhappy murmurings of people queuing in front of me, the officials were rude and intolerant. In all my travels, I couldn't think of an entry to a country which was more foul-smelling. Immediately I went to the office of immigration, I was then sent to the bank.

'You change money first and you no come back until you change, understand?' The bank was on the other side of a square space, a couple of hundred yards from edge to edge. The bank stank of chicken shit. The teller's *djellebia* was stained with couscous, like babies' dribble.

'Give me money,' he said with a smirk, 'give me £100, and you fill in form.'

'But I'm only going to be in your

country for two days,' I protested. He looked at me blankly and then smirking again he shoved a grubby piece of paper at me. 'When finished, go to custom men.'

There was nothing I could do against the dirty face of this bureaucracy. I pushed my bike across an area rutted by the tyres of heavy trucks.

'Good, you have form,' and a dark green uniformed Immigration official handed me yet another form to fill in and present to customs. It was very dark as I pushed my bike over to a bench acting as the customs post.

'This form, no good,' and the customs official waved me in the direction of Immigration. I returned to Immigration.

'Custom people, very stupid,' and an unshaven man there gave me another form to fill and represent to customs. Three hours after introducing myself to this forgotten outpost of Syria, I was eventually allowed into the country itself. In the middle of the night I cycled on the road to Damascus.

That night I rode for a further four hours which added another 50 miles to the total. The accurate mileage would have to be worked out again when I got home. Although I knew the distances between major cities around the world, I couldn't account for changes of route with exactness, but I considered a five per cent margin of error over the total distance of over 13,000 miles, about 650 miles, to be acceptable. However, I was conscious of the need to verify the world record. In the middle of the night it was difficult to actually verify the distance I claimed to have cycled, but during the day I stopped wherever I could to have someone sign my diary.

Having snatched a few hours' sleep, I woke up to find the sun blazing in my eyes. It was 7 a.m., and I'd overslept. It was 150 miles from where I'd woken up to the capital of Syria, Damascus. It was hot and by mid-morning the temperature had risen to 30°C. The road to Damascus was in excellent condition. It was also just about the only tarred road that existed in an area four-fifths the size of the United Kingdom. Perched on the edge of the awesome Syrian Desert, I was subjected to every truck, bus, van, car, jeep, and donkey journeying north to south that had managed to scrounge some fuel.

There was a robust cheerfulness about Syrian people which prevented the harsh realities of their life from becoming easily apparent. But here and there, a pouting child held out a thin scabby hand. Having, on a previous journey here, had encounters with some of the friendliest people imaginable, I knew it would only be a matter of time before a genuinely warm welcome would be extended. Plodding on through the morning, stopping only for water, I had the road and midday all to myself. The temperature continued to rise and early into the afternoon I guessed it to be over 35°C. As the early afternoon passed by, I made good progress. Being acclimatised to the heat, I felt strong. I was losing less water and my skin was sufficiently tanned to slow down the burning process of the sun, but something wasn't quite right. Another ten miles passed, and although I'd drunk plenty of water, I began to feel dizzy. I tried to continue, but was in fear of falling off the bike. Placing a foot down to steady myself I somehow missed the ground and fell. I didn't fall heavily, but after around 3,500 miles it came as a bit of a surprise. Something in a very confused mind told me to be careful. The side of my left thigh was grazed and one of my elbows was bleeding. My head throbbed and my body began to ache. I told myself that it was only heat exhaustion and with rest I'd be alright. Having ridden 100 miles since dawn, I had another 70 yet to do. I had no time to rest. With difficulty I remounted the bike and started to ride. The heat was unceasing and there wasn't any shade. I had to carry on. Suddenly I became aware of each pedal turn grinding. I could almost hear the ball bearings slide, hot metal in grease. I imagined the workings of my body beginning to slow down and when I saw the roadside stumble along at walking pace, knew it was more real than imaginary. Offering no resistance to a body that was now exhausted, I stopped cycling and dismounted. The bike fell to one side as my legs gave way. My injured left knee hit a hot white rock and my head struck a tree. The final moments of a collapse always seem to be in slow-motion. I knew I'd be alright because I simply couldn't believe the journey would fail. But I could be wrong. My stomach contracted and pushed. From my shoulders down, I shook. My stomach forced me to grip my sides and I was sick. I could have felt as ill on any street corner on any late Friday night, but lying alone on the edge of a desert, it somehow felt worse. Basking in the heat, the contents of my stomach stank. The sun tore relentlessly at my head, my arms, and my sore twitching legs. For the briefest of moments I didn't care whether I kept up with my schedule or not. Oh, but it would be so hard to fail. So with effort, I stood up shakily and climbed onto the bike. Everything in my vision was white. The longer I stood up, the more shape I managed to comprehend. A small village of white sun-baked clay houses stood, as if waiting for me. I hadn't noticed them before. I staggered towards them, half dragging, half wheeling my bike.

A couple of lads were seated by a small house that doubled as the soft drinks store. My throat was too parched to speak. I pointed to a bottle of Coke and it was opened. The drink was too cold to drink quickly, only by sipping it slowly I prevented my stomach from convulsing. The lads seemed to understand how I felt and politely waited until I was ready to talk.

'Thank you,' I said, 'I was not feeling well.'

'It is the desert,' said a young fellow with a mop of black hair, 'it can kill.'

'Perhaps you would do us the great honour of returning to my mother's home, something to eat perhaps, a little rest?' A tall fellow stood up and took me by the hand. 'Come, you are very tired.'

We wandered slowly in the heat, which without wind was breathtaking. The taller of my new aquaintences was called Hussein, the one with a mop of unruly black hair, Hamid.

After taking off our shoes in a pretty and enclosed back garden, we entered Hussein's private room. A younger brother, Karim, came in with a bowl of warm water and after a carpet had been laid, my hands were gently washed. The high ceiling was typical of homes in the Middle East, it had a remarkable cooling effect, and in a very short while I began to realise how the sun had affected me.

'Are you alright?' Hussein asked me. I nodded without conviction.

'Perhaps some water?'

'Thank you.'

Allowing me a few moments to gain my composure, three young men and a couple of friends arranged themselves in a circle, leaning back against the wall. Noticeable only to myself I began to shake. The heat of the sun had begun to soak me up from the inside. Feeling a little self-conscious I asked for five minutes to write my diary. I could hide behind words I could hardly write.

Day 21: On the road to Damascus

I am a little disturbed. I know. I cannot return home feeling like this. I am nervous. I am confused. I feel as if I'm experimenting with myself. I am not ready or able to go home yet. Whether it be this journey or the next, I sit here waiting for something wonderful to happen and the only unusual event today was me throwing up.

In the centre of the ceiling there hung a naked light bulb on a long piece of flex. It had gathered dust during the long hot summer. Hussein switched on a small tape recorder and we listened at first in silence to 'On The Road To Babylon'. It was an apt song but I wasn't listening to the words. With great pride, Hussein showed me his bowl of plastic fruit, imported specially from Europe. In a glass cabinet, by a well padded single bed, a row of bone china cups caught my eye.

'Ah yes, tea from an English cup,' said Hussein, speaking for the first time, 'now we can pretend to be gentlemen.' From many other countries, such a mock jest would be thought barbed. Here, it was said without malice.

'We are very honoured to serve you as our guest,' said Hamid, colouring slightly, 'we must look after you until you are ready to leave,' and the others nodded in agreement.

Hussein, having asked to leave the room, returned bearing a large shiny tray of the most sweet smelling foods.

'We have eggs, and spring onions, dhal which you must eat with your hand, and my mother made fresh yoghurt only yesterday. Come, after we

pray, we eat.' The chant of the Koran rested me, and coming from such an innocent source, was all the more pleasant.

During the course of our meal, a lively conversation ensued.

'Do you believe in God?' Hussein asked.

'Which one?' I said, knowing how unshakable their faith was and the predictability of their reply.

Hussein looked puzzled, 'but there is only one God.'

'What do you think about marriage?' said Hamid, 'do you believe in that?'

I sensed a certain credulity in their questioning. These young men had an innocence often lost in boys of their own age in the West. I asked Hamid if he had a girlfriend and if he had heard of the Rolling Stones.

'If it is that you are referring to the popular music,' he said, sitting up, 'I have just the very thing,' and reaching over to a small cassette machine, slotted in a cassette. In the dusty charm of Hussein's private bedroom, we listened to the sound of a woman breathing heavily. It sounded familiar.

'It is French, you know,' said Hussen, 'Jin Beerkin, "Je T'Aime", do you know it?'

'In a manner of speaking,' I said, and smiled.

Hamid had heavy eyebrows and was in the process of growing a moustache. His eyes were a little close together, and his lips a little thick.

'My English *in situ* is not good,' he said, 'we do not meet people like you too often.' The fan whirred above. Outside, the mosquito zapper blazed with morsels of flesh that an instant previously had the audacity to fly. For a moment I thought of Dad, sitting in his living room with his hands wrapped around his ankles. In the same way he would be thinking about me, straining over my handlebars. Feeling so much better, it was sadly time to go. Hussein bade me to stay and in such quiet unassuming company I would have preferred nothing better. I asked him to write to me at my hotel in New York and at that he handed me a bag of food prepared by his mother.

The worst of the heat had passed and I felt good and refreshed. Having ridden for eight hours, I only had another five or six hours yet to do. South of Homs, the road trembled with armoured vehicles. Hundreds of militia units were heading in the direction of Lebanon. The border was less than four miles away. In the distance I thought I heard the muffled blast of shell fire, but it could have been a truck back firing. The nearer I came to Damascus, the busier the traffic, until on the very outskirts of the city, the road was a heaving cauldron of frantically scrambling trucks and camouflaged jeeps. This time there would be no stopping in Damascus, but last time I was feted with goodwill. I remember staying in the youth hostel and being introduced to members of the PLO. Here the organisation is revolutionary and supported by all. In a house by leafy suburbs, I was given tea and cakes whilst a high ranking officer assured me I was perfectly safe. On leaving, I was given a wooden plaque cut out in the shape of Palestine, the officer inscribed the back in ink:

To my friend Nick,
This is the map of my homeland, Palestine. We were driven out from our land by force and threat. The Israelis, backed by the Zionists and Americans have contributed to the tragedy of the Palestinians. But neither poverty nor exile will suppress our longing for Palestine.

It was getting dark, and as I stopped to ask the way to the Jordan road, a taxi pulled up beside me and a pale plump woman suggested she be of assistance. 'I am Jordanian, if you go to Amman, you must go to see my husband. He will look after you.' Directing the taxi, she told me to follow her and in this way led me to the Jordan side of town. Scribbling a number on a piece of paper, she thrust it to me and I stuffed it somewhere in one of my bags.

Alone, on the road to Amman, I rolled out my sleeping bag and climbed inside. I was excited. Looking up to the stars, I couldn't help but feel like a little boy on the eve of a surprise. As the moon began to leave its horizon and edge up to its zenith, its fullness that night lit up the sandy landscape with fantasy. I knew something was going to happen, because gazing into eerie shadows I became aware of my churning stomach. I had a feeling that whatever might happen was no longer under my control.

On the early morning road to Jordan, I realised that a quarter of the journey had been completed. It was definitely a good enough reason to celebrate, so freewheeling into the parking area of a dilapidated old café, I asked the elderly waiter for breakfast.

Several well-scrubbed wooden tables lined the edge of a large central area that housed the kitchen. A cloud of smoke hung around the roof, eeking out through gaps where you could see the sky. On offer were eggs, eggs, or eggs. The crinkled waiter told me that the butcher had not delivered today, and neither had the vegetable man. He, the waiter told me, had run off with the butcher's wife, and the reason eggs were always in profusion was because the egg man was rather keen on the butcher, and they both contrived to deliver on a Thursday.

'It is like ze Hardy Rocky café in *Dallas* on ze television,' the waiter informed me as he scooped three eggs from his pan, 'you are having no need to go to ze Hollingwood, we are having ze same thing all of it off here....'

Having sat next to the cafés only window, I noticed wandering scrub being chased by the wind. Usually the scrub chases me. Separated by six rectangular panes of glass, it was like watching a silent movie. There didn't seem to be any relationship between me and what was happening outside. Similarly, I suppose, my cycling past the most faraway villages in the most faraway places must be as real to the people who see me as the characters on their cinema screen.

Breakfast had lasted twenty minutes and now I was anxious to get through the Jordanian customs. After an hour's cycling I approached the dirty buff-coloured building of Syrian customs. There I queued with a room full of lorry drivers thrusting their travel documents at a row of dark blue uniformed customs officials. Handing in my passport, I then expected to wait all morning before it was returned. After an hour, someone touched me on my shoulder and one of the officials handed me my passport and said I could proceed to the Jordanian customs. Three miles further on I was warmly welcomed by a group of young soldiers, immaculately dressed. I was technically in Jordan but still had to pass through immigration and customs, and they went further along the route. With luck, things should run smoothly and riding into the border bay, I was an innocent abroad about to face the most agonising moment of the journey so far.

As I presented my passport to a rather burly immigration official, he then proceeded to thumb its contents.

'You have travelled far,' he said, 'and where are you going?' Border checkpoints rarely expect the full truth when a brief account of the facts will suffice. I knew I was allowed overland into Israel, but I was also aware of the delicate political nature of such a crossing. Surrounding Arab countries believe Israel has no right to exist. Israeli people equally firmly believe the country is their promised land. This guard knew that the Jordanian-Israeli border can be crossed over the river Jordan but he might prefer to turn me away. I told him, Israel. He looked long and hard at me and remained silent and deathly.

'I think,' he said seriously, 'maybe, you can enter Israel from here.' I breathed a great sigh of relief which was not strong enough to dislodge the apprehension from my face. As I held out my hand, he closed my passport slowly and continued. 'There again, maybe you cannot.' I was stunned. 'You must return back the way you came and go from Greece,' and with that he handed me my passport and walked away. I felt sick. Not since the problem with the knee had I been flushed with such sweeping fear. It was moments like this which threaten so many hopes and destroy so many dreams.

Having crossed many borders, I knew that the more civil, westernised and organised the authorities, the more impossibly difficult the entry formalities. In India, border guards were often impossibly impolite; in Uganda, you were always told to come back after lunch; and in Sudan, no was as good as yes because everyone I met had that rather quaint appearance of not quite knowing what they were supposed to be doing. I sat down on a bench and tried to pull myself together. Should this problem not work out in my favour, the journey would be put in grave peril. There had to be a way around this because I was definitely within my rights to proceed. Sitting, watching, listening, I heard a woman shouting at a guard. She was a black lady dressed in the most eccentric manner. Electric blue flowers decorated a dress which flowed down to the dusty ground. Earrings, that probably doubled as bicycle-clips, dangled frantically from a very angry head. Someone shouted to me and looking up, another guard beckoned me forward.

'Please present your passport to desk D in the main hall and enquiries will be made to the appropriate source concerning your transit to Israel.' There was a chance. Waiting in line as telephone calls were made on my behalf, I watched every nuance of expression during the course of each telephone conversation. Standing behind me was the lady with the earrings.

'They are the svines of the world these Arabs,' she said to me knowing I was a foreigner and probably English-speaking. 'They vant to kill me, me and my poor ailing husband. They are the bastards.' Such was her anger, crimson showed even in her dark cheeks. The telephone calls continued and the voice on the other end caused a shaking of heads. I struggled to remain composed. Oblivious now to the scufflings in the large hall and distraught sounds from the woman behind me, I became aware only of the guard and myself.

'I vould curse them, all of them.' Jolted away from the telephone and the guard I turned to the woman. 'Why don't you just shut up, you're making it impossible for yourself?'

'Vat a qveustion you ask, but as you ask it. I will do as I wish. Perhaps now you would like to ask these dirty people a qveustion?' I turned away quickly. If the guards associated me with this woman, I would be in serious trouble. She didn't seem to want to be here, it wasn't surprising the Jordanians felt the same way about her. The guard summoned me to the front of the queue. I was sweating and such was my anxiety that I wanted to be sick. For a moment the guard paused.

'You may enter, the guard will rectify your visa and after customs, please proceed. You have seven days in Jordan. The bridge closes at 2 p.m.'

For that first official minute in the land where the King is nearly divine, I wanted to laugh and I wanted to cry. The journey, nearly thwarted by bureaucracy, had been allowed to continue. But there was another problem, just as serious as the one I'd overcome. It was 9.30 a.m. I had four and a half hours to cycle 80 miles, and only the last 20 were downhill, and they were to the deepest and one of the hottest lands in the world.

Straightaway, I jumped onto my bike, pedalling quickly away from the border, pushing round the pedals with all the spirit I could muster. Faster and faster I rode with the wind and Jordan appeared blurred. At first flat, the road began to descend and then undulated for an hour. By 10.45 a.m. I passed the town of Mafraq and then Jarash. Here, temples as old as the first act of geometry demanded my attention for a year, instead I could only give them 30 seconds as I pursued the King Hussein Bridge. By midday I was leaving the outskirts of Zarqa and less than an hour later, the beautiful splendour of Amman presented itself astride a mountain bejewelled by the whitest of sun-scorched rock.

Smartly dressed Ammanians had no intention of wading through the shifting sands of the desert wind which for miles around had been kept away. Winding between tall buildings of glass and chrome, roads as smooth as crystal mirrored me. I should have loved to stay longer but sped through in minutes. Everyone knew the way to the bridge so there was no chance of getting lost and after a couple of stiff climbs, I began the final ascent. It was 1 p.m. and I had 25 miles to go.

The air was hot and as I plunged into what felt like the centre of the earth, it would get hotter. Scraggy mountain goats licked clean the salt from rocks that stuck through sun-blasted brown earth. The sun was directly overhead as I raced faster. It was just possible the sun and I were the only things moving. Sinking down onto the bike frame I lowered my centre of gravity and smoothed myself against the resistance of the wind. Hurtling into and out of corners that were critically sharp and tight. I took a deep breath. Beads of sweat cooled the surface of my skin, only to evaporate into nothing. My face began to crease with the effort and the heat. My legs began to burn and blister and my throat was scaly. Neither car nor bus passed me from either direction but from the small garden of the occasional settlement a dog would hurl itself at my legs only to scour the road with blood and bone. I was almost in a frenzy. Chasing the wind to the valley of the Dead Sea gave me an altogether different perspective. Estimating my speed to be over 40 miles per hour, I whipped the wind around me. At such speed, a fall could be fatal but my desire outweighed the danger. It was 1.30 p.m. and there were ten miles to go. I'd ridden 130 miles since sunrise and it was beginning to hurt. The hurt wasn't like a cut finger that smarts, it was a dull ache that progressively becomes intolerable. Entering the last section of the descent I could feel the heat holding onto me.

Because the Israeli sabbath falls on a Saturday the bridge would be closed until Sunday and I would miss my scheduled flight from Tel Aviv to Athens. If I missed the connecting flight to Bombay the journey would effectively be over. Signposts marked 'King Hussein Bridge' indicated eight miles to go, then six miles and then four. A sentry guard waved me down and asked for my passport. He told me the bridge would be closed. It couldn't be, there were 15 minutes to spare. Jumping back onto the bike I made a last excitable effort to reach the bridge in time. The last mile was as straight as it was severe, and the land was barren as it was beautiful. The semi-arid landscape was nearly desert and except for air rising, nothing moved. At the end of the road the fertile valley floor was green and tropical, and over the river, the cinnamon brown of the Holy Land shimmered. Careering around a sweeping left-hand bend, I expected any moment to see the source of my little drama. With instant monumental disappointment, the shaky remains of an old army pontoon just about managed to span a gully that could house a river no bigger than a stream. One of the most politically sensitive and strategically important bridges in the entire world, looked as it had been nailed together from the bug-eaten remains of an old garden shed. A bus had just been allowed through the screened off area. It was still open. A youth dressed in combat uniform asked for my papers and I handed him my passport. He looked at me and said that wasn't enough.

'The papers, the papers, you must have the papers.' He was tense and when he saw that I didn't understand, he began to scream at me. I implored myself to remain calm. I didn't understand. No one ever mentioned special documents to me.

'You must have the papers, the bridge is closing, you cannot cross without the papers.' His machine gun glinted in the sun. In my own mind I had to interpret quickly what he was shouting. Had I not been to the Ministry of Defence for the special papers that would allow me to cross the bridge? Had I not the special permission required for all overland travel into Israel? Something was seriously wrong and I was getting confused. I asked to see his commanding officer and he obligingly disappeared into a small white building. It was five minutes to two. On the other side of the bridge, the blue star of Israel fluttered. Two Israeli gaurds shouted across to me, beckoning me towards them. For a moment I contemplated an act which would surely cause an international incident. I politely declined the offer. An older official emerged from the building.

'You cannot cross without the papers, it is quite impossible.' I pleaded my being a special case as I'm sure did everyone who arrived here as ill-informed. I was almost certainly the first cyclist to make such a crossing, didn't that mean anything to these people? I quickly chastised myself for such a stupid thought. Speaking into his walkie-talkie, he asked the Israeli guards what they thought about the situation. It had taken me four and a half hours to go full circle. The heat blazed, a thermometer on the wall of the building showed 45°C. The conversation continued and I closed my eyes. The tension was like a screw, but it couldn't have been tightened further. It was too much. A journey shouldn't be as hard as this. Slowly, the Israeli guards began to screen off their side of the bridge leaving a small gap uncovered. After a long pause in which my mind grappled with the unreality of this scene, the guard made a move. Turning to me, the official said he would overlook the papers. I could cross. I didn't believe what he was saying, the sun was affecting me badly. He urged me on. I began to push my bike towards the bridge. I felt ill, aggrieved even, that a journey from one country to another should be so desperately difficult. Slowly, as if trying to walk for the first time after an accident, I reached the first plank of the bridge crossing the River Jordan. Looking up, I couldn't believe what I saw. The narrow gap in the screen, left open specially for me was now closed. I was too late. My journey around the world in 80 days had just been determined by a technicality. Turning my face away from anyone who might see me, I stood alone, on the bridge, in the desert, and cried.

Soon afterwards I heard the sound of a bus. The elder of the two officials put his arm around my shoulders. 'I'm afraid you've got to leave the area,' he said gently, 'the bus is going back to the city and if you'd like a ride I can arrange it.'

I thanked him and nodded. It was all over. I loaded the bike onto one of the seats and sat back to watch the long snaking road. The features of this valley were somehow browner, second time around. Sheer cliff faces were toasted mahoghany and outcrops of rock had softened from white-hot to amber. A flock of white birds drifted peacefully above. I too wanted to fly away. The bus trundled and steamed, thumping great pistons hammering drive shafts to perform just one more revolution, and then another. It was cool in the shade and, with the windows open, it would have been decidedly more pleasant to have gone around the world in a bus. Dusted down and watered in the coolness of a shadow I remembered certain original objectives of my attempt to cycle around the world. For the last five years I'd been working at acting out my dreams and had no idea how to conduct my life differently. The first journey around the world, subsequent journeying in Asia, and the journey to the source of the Nile, where I stood 6,000 feet high on the Burundi Hills overlooking the heart of Africa, were the crowning of a little personal glory. I decided that even if I did not achieve the record, my other journeys existed quite well in their own right. There was no point in worrying about defeat when circumstances were against me because there was nothing else I thought I could do as well.

The bus pulled in to a small street in the centre of the old city of Amman and I climbed out and thanked everyone for being so helpful. I told the official we'd meet again on Sunday. He smiled and I cycled off to mingle with a street full of people and wait for whatever was to happen next.

Finding a money changer I suddenly remembered the lady in Damascus, she had given me the telephone number of her husband, perhaps he could help me? Rummaging through my bag, a slip of screwed up paper fell onto the floor. The man who dealt me my Jordanian money connected the call and spoke on my behalf. If I stood by the Post Office, the lady's husband would collect me in half an hour. He would surely know the various procedures I would have to follow if I were to try and

cross the bridge on Sunday. Almost to the minute, a grey Mercedes pulled up and the boot of a car raised automatically. Quickly dismantling the bike I did what was necessary and jumped into the car.

Mr Mousaki was a short, portly man, heavily jowled and never without a cigarette belching from his lips. Judging by his movements, I would say he strongly adhered to the law of conservation of energy. If it wasn't for the fact that he was driving a car, I would suggest he wasn't moving at all. So far he hadn't spoken a word, and as we pulled into the driveway of a large building I presumed to be his house, it occurred to me he might not speak English. The door of the car opened automatically and after pressing a control unit so did a solid oak front door leading to a reception hall. Still without speaking he led me to my room and escorted me to the bathroom, handing me a towel.

'You will be requiring this,' he said, passing me some soap.

'Oh, you do speak English,' I said, immediately biting my lip for being so obvious.

'I do my business in Jordanian, I sometimes teach in French, I read ancient Hebrew, and speak Greek, Italian, German and Spanish fluently.' He paused, 'and I also speak English'. Lingering, he gave me a last glance and allowed me to wash.

Dinner was a Kentucky fried chicken brought back by one of his sons which I ate in the company of Mr Mousaki who had closed his eyes to rest. He was a strange man, not exactly the most humorous of human beings, and his replacing one cigarette for another was the only indication he was awake. Nevertheless, I now had time to think and tomorrow I would go to the Ministry of Defence and try and sort out this mess. Passing me a second box of fried chicken he considered it necessary to speak.

'I do not indulge in idle chit-chat. Life is too short to be immersed in such pathetic inconsequentialities. The whole of mankind reveres rubbish and the martyrdom of makeshift thought, what do you think?'

'I don't.'

'What do you mean?' He said looking puzzled, 'you don't what?'

'I don't think while I'm eating.'

Intellectual onslaught was a fine distraction but I had ridden 150 miles in the sun and gratuitous Kentucky fried chicken was insufficient incentive to encourage this form of interrogation.

'I want to know how people's minds work and I must probe fresh spirit at every God given opportunity, please do not be offended.' He remained quiet for some time, having realised this new spirit didn't give up its secrets easily. Every time I've returned home from an adventure, the need to share the experience increases and the ability to do so decreases. I always knew that if such free-spirit becomes trapped in one person, the key to understanding becomes jammed.

'Do you mind if I ask you a personal question,' he said, as if starting from a slumber. He could ask what he wanted. Taking a few moments to continue, as if to compose the question in a particular way, he looked directly at me. 'Have you ever had a relationship with a member of the same sex?'

'Don't think so,' I said without showing the slightest surprise. A long pause followed.

'Come now, you must know whether you have or you haven't. You do know what a member of the same sex is, do you not?' He laughed. A game was being played which would be enacted at my expense if I followed his rules and disregarded my own. I had three options; either I accept his proposition and prostitute myself, I leave and jeopardize a quick end to the bridge problem, or I react like a woman and deflect his attention from me. Trapped by the situation I had a feeling of repulsion, not specifically because of his attentions, but I resented being taken for granted.

'You are assumming of course that I've had a relationship with a member of the opposite sex, let alone my own kind.' There followed an even longer pause, he was uncertain now how he might continue.

'Er, have you ever wanted to...?'

'Wanted to... what?' I interrupted, remaining purposely obtuse. There was another long pause, but this time he shuffled from one elbow to another whilst replacing another cigarette.

'Has any man wanted to,' he paused, 'to have,' and scratching his chin, 'to have a relationship with you?'

'Don't know,' I said using a necessary economy of words and truth, 'what do you think?'

'I think, yes.' He waited for a moment and continued, 'I do not suppose you have had time for any sort of relationship riding whatever you do everyday?' That was so, but 'time' had nothing to do with the way I wanted to be alone, at least for the duration of this journey, and quickly I finished my chicken pieces.

'Could I trouble you for a cup of coffee?'

He looked stunned and then laughed out loud. I had guessed his little game and I took a deep breath.

'Young man, you are absurd.'

'So are you,' I said, and he smiled.

The room I was given was hot and stuffy, so climbing onto the flat roof I laid out my sleeping bag in full view of a city's twinkling lights. The wind was cool and blowing through nearby telephone wires it hummed a monotone lullaby that heightened with every gust.

The following morning, Mr Mousaki dropped me off by the steps of the Ministry for the Interior. Before midday I should receive the documents to continue the journey, during the course of the afternoon I would try to rearrange my flight to India and telephone the *Saturday Picture Show*. Sitting in room 34 I chatted to an army officer, who, judging by the number of decorations pinned to his uniform was very high ranking. In the middle of our conversation I was instructed to deliver a wad of notes to room 27. Having obtained the necessary signature, I was told to come back in three days by which time the paperwork would have been processed by the Ministry of Defence. Before his words had been untangled, a voice behind me said he'd sort them out personally and that I was to pick up the permission to cross at 12 p.m. That very same high ranking officer was actually concerned that the journey wasn't thwarted in Jordan. Maybe now my luck would change.

Amman was two hours ahead of Greenwich Mean Time so, having collected my papers, I dashed across the road to one of the international hotels and telephoned the BBC. Each week I still managed to relate my adventures to the audience back home. A film crew was to be made available to meet me on the West Bank of the river early Sunday morning, and a press conference had been arranged in the Jerusalem Hilton later that afternoon. Not crossing the bridge as planned had its small compensations. Having missed my Tel Aviv flight, I bought the last available

seat on a flight to Bombay from Cairo. As it departed at 6 p.m. on Monday, I would have to cross the Sinai in less than a day. Fortunately that wouldn't be a problem as I already knew a bus departed Jerusalem in the morning and arrived in Cairo at 4 p.m. Should the bus not be running, I could be really cool, and hire a taxi across the Sinai Desert. I had been told by the *Guinness Book of Records* before I started this journey that under such circumstances such route changing was justifiable as long as I didn't include the mileage in the journey. Cycling around the world isn't like running around an athletics track, it's more like an obstacle course where other skills come into play as well as speed and endurance. Also, this was the only time that the adventure journeyed west, every other moment of the 80 Days was in an easterly direction.

The following morning I rose before sunrise to begin the journey to the bridge. It was becoming a strange journey. One moment I was destitute on the bridge, the next, preparing to ride across it, all smiles in view of a camera lens. As the sun began to rise, the descent became warmer. I remembered a film I had once seen, *The Purple Rose of Cairo*. Mia Farrow is the hard done by spouse of a drunken loafer and her sole pleasure in life is found at the local movie house. Over and over again she sees *The Purple Rose of Cairo*, a highlife comedy in which, due to her absorbtion in the movie, a pith-helmeted explorer, Tom Baxter, comes alive and strolls causually off the screen. Maybe my absorbtion with my journey would produce such a meeting, after all, this adventure had hurt and I wanted the pain to be soothed. More importantly, there were ten miles to go. As if to savour the moment of glory, I sat and munched biscuits in a tea house at the four-mile post. The bridge for a second time came into view and I, sweat-stained and slightly torn apart by the floundering of the journey, waved to the camera crew to be ready as I crossed.

Having missed the morning bus across the Sinai, it didn't really matter that the filming lasted eight hours. George was the camaraman and Abrahem was the sound recordist. After the filming had finished, we drove to my hotel and ordered a drink each at the bar. The Front Desk Manager came over to speak to me. 'I have reserved you a seat on the bus to Cairo, you must leave at 6 a.m. tomorrow. There are also some Press to see you,' he pointed to a far corner of the bar where a group of people were seated. Excusing myself from the film crew I then related my story so far to the Press. Twenty minutes later I was back at the bar. George had not been idle, 'one every five minutes,' he said holding up what looked like a gin and tonic. I certainly didn't have time to get to know Israel but in the short time that I was there, had become aware of the humour that can survive during a state of war. 'There was something in the paper that made me laugh out loud,' George said to me. 'This country of ours is so skint, a judge has ruled that burglars must declare their income on their annual income tax returns or face the consequences. Can you imagine that?' Abrahem remained quiet as George ordered another drink. 'This thief was fined 50,000 shekels for not declaring his earnings.' George screamed with laughter and tired though I was, started to laugh myself.

'He fell from the first floor window of a flat he was attempting to rob, he landed on the pavement opposite a police station and broke his hip. What a story.' By this time George and I were laughing so much that we had to hold on to the bar to stand up. Abrahem said he had heard the story before. Tears were streaming down George's cheeks.

'The defendant testified that he had now given up his life of crime, bloody liar, he'll have ended up in the bazaar.' When Abrahem suggested it was time to go, George nodded but said he had to be helped to his car. Still laughing, we said goodbye and I decided to head for my room.

In the lobby, 600 women from the Jewish Singles Association had flown from America for their annual convention and lookabout. Normally I would have been like a little boy in a candy store, but then I had about enough strength to pick up a newspaper. A letter published in the *Jerusalem Post* from a disgruntled female tourist reminded me that the predatory women were likely to be disappointed.

'When I arrived in Israel from Sweden six months ago, one of the first things I noticed was the way you drive here. It is a common belief in my country that a man drives a car in much the same way as he makes love to a woman. When I saw all these drivers without any feeling whatsoever for driving, doing the most stupid things, I laughed to myself and thought I knew another thing people here were not very good at.

After six months here, I don't laugh any more. It is true – Israeli men make love in the same way they drive and this is neither a pleasant nor a satisfactory experience for a woman. To prove my point, it is a well-known fact that a large proportion of Israeli women are overweight. I will not reveal how many kilos I gained during my stay here, but I am a living accusation against Israeli men.

The following morning I loaded my bike on to the roof of the bus, and it wasn't long before the patchy desert of the Sinai replaced the biblical Judean hills which wound down to the Gaza strip. The last two days had played havoc with my 171 mile daily average, but at least the journey was still alive and the world record was still a possibility. Because I was reducing my previous record of a 138 days to 80 days, I didn't envisage any problems in getting a slightly lower mileage ratified. I hoped that by lowering my record by 57 days would be such an improvement, the fact that I might not cycle around the world quite as far as before would not present a problem. As I had originally intended to fly from Tel Aviv anyway, I regarded my taking a bus ride to Cairo as the only way to continue. The mileage would not be counted therefore it was not to be included in the record and it was justifiable.

As I headed west for the first time since the journey began, barren sands danced in the wind to remind me of the first time I crossed the Sinai. In the March of '81 it was a hot Spring and I took three days to ride from Cairo to Jerusalem. I'll never forget the dogs of the night. It was bleak and during the day there existed not a moment of shade. Even the Bedouins had scarpered to the desert edge and I sauntered into the sun without a care in the world. Throughout the day I heaved round the pedals to the tune of the wind and as an afternoon storm began to push and thrust, that tune became a sky scraping me with sand. Wrapped up tight as a mouse in a nest I hid in my cape, and crouched behind a dune to stand my ground against a battering. The storm didn't abate until the influence of the sun was shielded by the horizon and as evening fell, the desert became silent. Never before had I known a quietude where the loudest sound within shouting distance would be the beat of my own heart. That silence was broken by the bloody howls of a pack of wild dogs. Even the wind sobbed and sighed in the dead of night, and had they known of my whereabouts, I felt sure they wouldn't have hesitated to fight over the scrawny pickings of a body that had been pulled to pieces, screaming in the darkness. I stayed awake all night in fear.

After an eight hour bus ride, I smelled the rancid stink of a city on the move. Scrambling to the hotel, I had two hours to meet a few journalists, pick up my mail, and dine briefly with the manager. Throwing the bike onto the roof of a taxi we honked and charged our way to the airport, past Heliopolis on the very far side of the city. The traffic of Cairo was depravity itself, but never did I see more than a shaking angry exchange. In the quietness of the bullock-pulled, ploughladen Nile delta, Cairo was an abomination. It reeked of perfume and it stank of shit. Housing some of the finest treasures the world will ever know, it incarcerates them in the filthiest, most scummy, slatternly, suppurating untidiness that can exist, and for every greasy, grimy stick and stone, I loved her more than words could tell. If Cleopatra wanted to be 'blown into abhorring in flyblown slime,' I suggest she do it here. Reluctantly leaving the Middle-East, I jumped onto my flight to India.

5 · INTO ASIA

It was *Day 25* and the flight to Santa Cruz airport in Bombay took me into the early morning of *Day 26*. At least for the duration of the flight, I could rest in relative comfort. I liked flying.

Normally I sleep when flying but sitting next to me was a man from England.

'I'm a community worker from Manchester,' he said introducing himself, 'I've been planning this trip for three years and it's been in my head for ten years.' Peter had a kind warm face with wrinkles around eyes that allowed for lots of smiling. He also had raised eyebrows, a characteristic I associated with listening. 'I've been in Turkey these past two months. It's a great place. If you ever go, try and get to the underground city around Capadocia.'

'I've spent three days in Turkey,' I told him, 'and saw nothing but the open road.'

He raised his eyebrows, listening in disbelief. As he smoked a cigarette, he looked at me apprehensively. 'Do you

think India will live up to my dreams. Is it really full of poor people and lepers?'

'Its a beautiful country, the people are friendly in a way that doesn't exist in the West.' I paused before giving him a gentle warning. 'Do be careful. What is only a day's spending money to you is a week's wages to some people. In the wrong place at the wrong time you could be killed.'

I, too, was concerned about the Indian section of the journey. The sheer enormity of the country with her 700 million people is part of the experience. My apprehension was composed of love and loathing; to love the feeling of excitement, adventuring in foreign lands, and to loathe the inevitable feeling of a stomach clogged up with 'butterflies'.

'Waiting in the departure lounge I was with a girl who was so nervous she could hardly hold her cigarette.' He pointed her out to me and I turned around to look at her. her lips were quivering and when she saw me, she gave me a frightened smile.

'I got this letter from me Mum,' Peter continued, 'a thousand words it was, asking me why I don't settle down and stop this larking about.' He paused for a second, 'I wrote back suggesting her life was boring and tedious with a husband she hasn't spoken to properly for thirty years.'

'I've been trying to tell the kids on television that they could bike around the world if they wanted to,' I said, 'but I may have underestimated the difficulties.'

'I showed my Indian visa to an Indian lad in Brixton,' he added, 'and he

didn't even know where India was, so what's the point in saying he could bike around the world?'

For a moment I was silent. I felt so sick I couldn't speak.

'What's the matter?' he asked, 'you've gone white.'

'I haven't got a visa,' I said, only too aware of the dreadful implications for my journey.

When the British colonised India, visas were not required. After Independence in 1947, any British passport holder could reside there unconditionally for 49 years.

'It's the Sikhs,' he said, 'they've been relying on their British passport to get in and cause trouble, new legislation, very recent.' What happened in Jordan could happen all over again, this was crazy, I thought that I had prepared for this trip so well. It was Robbie Burns who said, 'the best laid plans of mice and men aft gang agley,' and he was so right.

'They could lug you back to Cairo,' Peter said helpfully, brushing his stubbly chin. 'A friend of mine hadn't got a visa and they locked him up for five days until they got it all sorted out.'

Four years ago, the first time I'd stepped out from the confines of Bombay's international airport, a portion my hair was last seen disappea down the gutter of a dusty street. ing in the dark early hours of a morning it was considered d for me to cycle before exhausted, I stretched out the arrival hall and slep thing tugging at my h with bleary eyes I rem moist nose of a larg pressed for just a own. The hair sh like mine and before

what rightfully belonged to me, she turned tail and skidaddled with the prize clenched between murky brown teeth. Entering the airport now for the second time I waited nearly an hour in the queue for foreign passport holders. Something was going to go very seriously wrong.

'You are not having a visa,' the immigration official said sternly.

I explained what a mistake I'd made and how important it was for me to be in India, that I'd only be in the country for eight days. Seated behind a creaking wooden table he looked like a schoolboy not quite the right size for his desk.

'The visa situation for British passport holders has changed, you cannot enter, you must continue your journey immediately to Calcutta.' The roar of an aircraft filled the hall and a colleague informed him that the flight to Calcutta had just taken off. 'Then he must be going back to Cairo, quite immediately.' I was taken quietly aside and after what seemed an interminably long wait that was probably no longer than hour, I was allowed to explain my problem to various levels of officials.

ied to explain to the Indian offiilly we all might appear if we
an amicable coma full hour and a
he Head of Airport
it was in his interests
y into India.

The official replied, 'but
e doing this to everyone.
thics to consider, not forgetid and organised pattern of
ehaviour. You have transgress.' He paused. There is a time to
e and a time to agree or say
hing, I thought to myself. I
emained silent.

'But, I will make an allowance just

61

this once.' He considered himself to have exercised his authority in the manner that befitted a head of department. So reprimanded, I expected to be given a visa straightaway. 'Now it is such that we are having to impound your passport, it will be taken to the Police Commissioner's Office, Section Two of the CID in Crawford Market where you must convince the authorities of your eligibility to enter. You may go.'

'But my passport, you know what it's like, it'll get lost,' I blurted, immediately wishing I'd said nothing.

'How dare you,' and the Head of Airport Immigration inflated his chest like a peacock. 'Your passport will be taken directly. I will hear none of this. Now go,' and he turned round and strutted away.

Now I could roam around India without a passport, and that seemed a contradiction of the logical process which allows aliens into a country.

It was 5 a.m. Indian time. It was dark and outside grey rats scurried around a lighted lamp. The road into Bombay goes south and I would have to cycle north out of the city on my way to Calcutta. The bureaucratic fight I was to face required all my energy and so I loaded my bike onto the roof of a taxi and settled down to a bumpy six mile ride. As the driver turned on the ignition, a beggar woman pressed her face and scrawny breasts against the nearside window. In her hands were a bundle of rags and when I looked closer I saw the features of a baby. In the early morning light it looked blue. It could have been dead or alive. I turned away, my hands clenched in anger that this should be allowed to happen.

As the taxi bumped along I remember reading that every day 1,500 more people arrive in Bombay looking for somewhere to live and some form of work. If they are lucky, they find work as street sweepers, picking up cigarette ends to recycle into a new cigarette. 'Ten dog-ends' I was told would create something that was saleable. Lepers and peasants hung around the bustling streets, occasionally squabbling over a dropped rupee. At night, they join the 100,000 people sleeping on those same pavements, covering their heads with sacking and plastic sheeting, their pathetically small bundles of pots and clothes beside their skinny bodies as they try to sleep before the noisy city wakens them to another day of hard work and meagre wages.

Bombay wasn't quite awake when we arrived near the city centre so I directed the taxi driver to Haji Ali where I could get a cup of coffee from my old friend the doctor. Doctor Wirshakter found me moping in a corner café here four years ago. I was trying to find the road to Delhi on the India leg of the first journey and was hopelessly lost. He was a quietly authoritative man and insisted I spend the night at his house. At twenty-three I had never travelled further east than the outskirts of Paris and it felt a little strange sitting cross-legged on the floor eating foods I thought only grew out of packets. I remember how, after dinner, he put his arm around me and we went onto a balcony that looked over a beautiful racecourse. Even though he knew me but a few hours, I was to be like a son to him. And for his own son, I was to be a mystical uncle from far away. Whenever I should return, a cup of my favourite milky sweet coffee would be waiting. We arrived and I paid the taxi-driver his fare. For Bombay standards this area was quite well off, yet there were beggers and urchins on every street corner. The Doctor greeted me with no surprise, it was as if he knew who I was but couldn't quite remember where he'd seen me before. I was quite shocked. I had good acquaintances in various cities around the world, one of whom was the Doctor. He said very little at first and then clasped his hands and looked grave.

'Do you remember the last time you were here I lent you 100 rupees.' It was four years ago and although until then I had actually forgotten, I distinctly remember it being a gift. 'Well I'm a bit hard up this week and I was wondering if you'd mind...' I paid the money and sat in silence for another ten minutes.

Knowing someone in a faraway place gave me a feeling of security. They would explain the basics of survival in their own country and I could proceed with a greater chance of success. I left the Doctor feeling empty and hurt by his indifference towards me. Saying goodbye, I decided to save time trying to direct myself to Crawford Market and took another taxi-ride. It was 8.30 a.m. and Bombay was bursting at the seams. Smokey old buses covered everybody with soot and taxis honked incessantly. Before going to the Police Commissioner's office I decided to go to the British Embassy for advice. After all, I would be only one of hundreds that day who had done something really stupid.

Compared to the silence of the desert, the noise of the city was unsettling. In the desert at night there was often nothing at all to hear apart from the sounds of your own body. Here there was no pattern to the sounds which pounded on fragile windows and broken walls. Pulling up to a set of lights I became aware of the city becoming quiet. So as to save every thimbleful of petrol the driver had switched off his engine, and when I looked up, so had everyone else. For a moment this part of the city of Bombay was quiet. In the rear window of a taxi slightly in front of me, the sky was reflected, across which there flew a flock of birds. As they edged their way to the curved far side they became elongated and their motions seemed slower. A patch of blue sky showed so perhaps the monsoon would be less heavy. As the sounds of engines starting and policemen's whistles drifted back into my senses, the traffic lights turned green.

The First Secretary of the Embassy wrote a letter testifying to my character and wished me well. At least there was somebody out there who liked me. Having accomplished my errand I made my way to Crawford Market, and waited under the verandah of the Police Commissioner's Office. Looking over a courtyard full of scrambling children and dogs, a breeze whispered around tired green ivy hanging around off-white flaking pillars. I waited. I knew that if I was impeccably diplomatic, this unforseen hitch might go away. If it wasn't resolved, I might as well wait forever. The journey would have been brought to a premature end by the interminable delay of India's notoriously archaic and lethargic bureaucracy. So I sat and waited. I thought how apt was that epitaph of Rudyard Kipling: 'Here lies a man who tried to hurry the East.'

I remembered once meeting the Honorable Consul General of Ireland for Bombay in his suite in the Royal Bombay Yacht Club. He was a most delightful man whose business card introduced him as 'Callaghan of India'. He claimed a letter so addressed would reach him from anywhere in the world. I once wrote to him from home, and it was promptly returned from Ostend, stamped 'Address Unknown'. Sitting under delicate whirling fans that echoed against the refined leathered cloisters of his study, he had confided to me his idea of understanding India.

'There are 700 million people in India and you get to know a country by knowing its people. Consider this; if you know one per cent of that population you must know 7 million people. Impossible. A tenth of one per cent is 700,000, and one hundreth of one per cent is still to know 70,000 of the people of India. I have lived here twenty-four years, travelled all over every state, and dealt business in the village hall and at ministerial level in the National Congress. I barely know 70, and I don't know the country.'

'We are having to play the game,' the assistant Police Commissioner explained, startling me from my thoughts of Callaghan back to an awareness of the present and his dusty files, adding rhetorically, 'what would we do if we didn't?'

My passport was in front of him, which was in itself a surprise. It lay agonisingly close to his pot of purple ink. For a moment we faced each other across the desk, me silently willing him to give me the clearence I so desperately needed.

'Well I am supposing in this instance we could be tempted to be making an exception, but as you are obviously making intentions to be habiting to cycling around this world, I suggest the exception that we are making, be heeded in the strongest terms, that whenever you come to India again, you are having the appropriate visas,' he continued pompously, thumping the vital permit onto my documents with a flourish, which indicated that he had enjoyed having me in his power for long enough. Placing the passport into my saddlebag, I breathed a sigh of relief. It was midday and I had eight days to ride around 1,500 miles across the Indian sub-continent to Calcutta.

I took the route out of Bombay pedalling against the oven-hot wind.

By mid-afternoon I was in a country decorated no longer by the corrupted city. Scarves and ribbons flapped in the wind, bent-backed farmers pulled out strands of rice. The conditions for cycling here were good because the hot sun was obscured by monsoon clouds which were beginning to dry and roll away. I would follow the rains or they would follow me. India is no hotter than the Sinai or the Nubian Desert, but her scorching winds increase the heat factor to an unbearable degree, and in the stillness of an afternoon, in anticipation of a deluge, I could fly past rice paddies, green and beautiful. Before the road became awash with heavy drops of rain, I drank *chai* from village food vendors and peeled boiled eggs to eat as I rode. Camping equipment would have weighed me down and as food vendors are never more than a village away there was no need to cook for myself. Having been on the road for nearly half of the last five years, I've eaten with hundreds of different street vendors, and never yet have I suffered from anything more than the occasional bowel parasite or a sickly stomach.

At this time of year you couldn't predict a dry night so I slept in small hotel rooms that charged less than a pound for a single room. For the first two days I was aware of little else other than my riding, sleeping and eating. *Day 26* deposited me well past the outskirts of Nasik, past the waterhole where I once bathed in the company of a group of boys and their snorting herd of water buffalo. *Day 27* witnessed a wonderfully cool westerly wind and another

190 miles was added to the total mileage as I ended up in the town of Akola in the state of Madhya Pradesh. I was tired. Before long I would run out of adjectives to describe my fatigue. I decided that I was tired throughout the day, on the verge of exhaustion at the end of the day, and only safe from my travail when asleep. Westerners journeying in India think I travel too fast, that I see nothing and understand even less. But I saw it differently than they did and experienced India in my own way. For me, the wonderfully magical, mysterious, erotic, experience of India is at its most beautiful from a distance. However, the limitations in cycling so quickly across such a vast continent allow me to gain only the most jaundiced of impressions. Cycling alone on a bicycle that cost enough to feed a family here for a year, puts me in the privileged position of a rich tourist in confrontation with people who have to bear the crippling unfairness of being poor. Four days after leaving Bombay I reached the outskirts of Nagpur. It wasn't a very big city but it was home for the night of *Day 29*.

As dusk formed, a jeep drove alongside me and an Indian businessman wanted to know if he could be of assistance, offering the use of his telex machine. Such was the coincidence, that I decided to telephone the *Picture Show* that night instead of spending wasteful hours trying to make the live studio the following day. Telephoning Britain from India is much less predictable than a call would be from home to Nagpur. So after locating a hotel in town with a telephone, I cycled over to the office of this fellow I'd known for half an hour. He kindly typed out the telephone number and a request for the 'Show' to call me in the hotel at 8 p.m. On a telex machine, a

signal indicates that the message has been sent and received and that meant I could return to the more mundane task of filling a hungry stomach and scraping off a day's gathered dust.

The shower was a hut on the roof of the hotel in which an old watering can was suspended from the ceiling. Into the can dribbled a non-stop flow of water and tethered at the spout, a piece of frayed sack-rope dangled. Pulling the rope caused icy water to fall as would rain, and with eyes closed, I could have been showering just as easily in the street. On releasing the rope the can would level, fill up with more water and the shower was again made ready. Someone rattled the shower room door.

'Mister Neek, I am having to tell you that it is man from BBC on telephone.' The phone call to the *Picture Show*. I'd forgotten it completely and here I was without a stitch of clothing. Grabbing in my panic the shower curtain which was the first thing that came to hand I ran down three flights of stairs where the receiver of the phone was waiting patiently. The studio sound engineer tested me for level and I asked the small chubby proprietor if he wouldn't mind switching off the hotel's air conditioning. In the studio, everyone was informed they were about to record, and in front of a live audience of two old men, a boy, a dog, and a goat in the Blue Diamond Hotel in downtown Nagpur, I spoke to three million television viewers whilst wrapped in a turqoise and pink saree dripping from the only shower I've had from a watering can. I knew I'd be famous one day. I'm now very well known in Nagpur.

The following morning, *Day 30*, I set off at 4 a.m. towards Durg on the river Raipur. The once dusty plains were presently green and luscious, the air was fresh and I had three days to cycle

700 miles. Then for once I could allow myself one day's respite.

By 6.30 a.m., I had ridden 40 miles but already the farm workers were tending to their plantations. These farmers, dotted all over in their blues and yellows and saffrons and reds, were bent double placing and picking their crop. The cost of grain and economics of labour make use of every inch of land and so precise is the geometry of the field it was an artform. It was breakfast time and I was like a greyhound, steaming in the early morning sun. A *chai* vendor passed me a clay cup in which he poured the most deliciously sweet carmine-coloured tea, and I sat and sipped, hearing only the trundling of passing ox-carts. I twitched with all the animality of an athlete at his starting block. The investment in bullock carts is equivalent to the total investment in the Indian Railways and the Indian Railways is the fifth largest employer of labour in the world. Costing as much as a second-hand car in England, carts are only for the richer peasants and even then the bullocks only lasted about three years. I suspect it was longer but the bullock had an odd shape and the ineffective harnassing with the yoke caused skin cancer and did in fact shorten the life of the animal. I noticed the field across the narrow road. Tall shoots of maize stood like soldiers in regimented rows. Where the field of maize allows the road to cross, woman squat and wash white enamel plates as morning fires heat up sooty black pans, sparks flying into the damp. Dogs stood motionless, watching themselves in puddles and little girls ran and skipped, their skin fresh and bright and as brown as powdered chocolate. I had stopped for half an hour. Until I was approximately south of Bilapia on the way towards the banks of the river Mahanandas, it proved to be the only stop of the day.

By *Day 31* I had ploughed through the bouncing rain in Pradesh and North Orissa, only to rest near the banks of the river Mahanadi. During *Day 32* I realised I was incapable of maintaining my diary, such was my fatigue. Past the Mahanandi, I vaguely remember riding through Rourkela and arrived in Jamshedpur in a state of some exhaustion. One very long 200 mile day separated me from my rest day in Calcutta, and as my clothes steamed on the radiator in my room on the outskirts of town, with nothing to say and even less to think, I slept until dawn.

Day 32: *On the road to Calcutta*
The rain falls on the corrugated roof of a hut selling chai. *A row of raindrops run*

66

down the window bars. Lightning flashes are followed at once by rolling thunder echoing fron cloud to cloud. I am in the epicentre of a storm. How comforting it is to hear rain drops land. Sometimes it's not easy to admit that being alone is hard and that there is no-one with whom I can share the anguish of the journey welling up inside me.

By the end of *Day 32* I hoped to be in Calcutta. The monsoon chased and approached me. From east Madhya Pradesh through north Orissa to the very eastern edge of India and West Bengal, I rode mostly in silence. Dripping in never-ending rain I sipped the occasional *chai* and licked my fingers clean of the warmest of curry-soaked chapatis. Roasted over an open fire, hot banana and chestnuts were delicious. As hungry hands wiped themselves against me I despaired for their thin,

sad little bodies. As I laughed and joked with the village elder under a tree, rustling with the coolness of a freshly blowing wind, I felt happier. The road was still good and the wind blew me east as if I'd been particularly favoured. I was so looking forward to reaching West Bengal where for a day I could rest. I was desperately tired. Mile after mile, I plodded, 15 miles per hour for 14 hours with two breaks of half an hour each. The time passed quickly and as yet another dusk began to fall, my fatigue increased. Sometimes as I cycled around the world, there was little else to think about, the journey, my exhaustion, where I should sleep and what I might eat. So another tiring day passed, another 219 miles, another 14 hours, before I was threading my way through the area of the Hooghly river and onto the massive iron Howrah Bridge. Today I had ridden 219 miles in the pouring rain. Clunking along metal plates in a lane separate to the steaming and smokey old buses, I rode into the richest, most industrialised, illiterate and poverty-stricken city between Athens and Singapore: Calcutta.

Under the eaves of roofs held together by a million nuts and bolts, naked children ate and played, shitted and slept. Fathers sewed patches on large canvas tarpaulins stretched along the pavement whilst mothers searched among rubbish with babies tied to their backs with rags. Here Victorian red-brick buildings stood, grimy and decayed, squalid as an old Manchester slum. The cobbles were as from Rochdale and the type-script on factory porches and doors from the same lettering mould as turn of the century English ledgers. Pedalling through the rain and into flooded streets, I crept past the burnt sienna facade of the city's commercial centre, south of which, a small weathered green plaque bore reference to the Black Hole. On the hottest night of 1756, June 25, the day before the monsoon, 146 people were crammed into the space of an 18-ft cube. With bodies pressed unbearably close, by six o'clock the following morning only 23 people remained alive.

My legs were strong with the day's effort and the added stimulus of the city gave me a feeling of elation. As I carried on past the High Court, across Dharantala Street and on to Chowringhee, I saw Indians wearing Western dress forging ahead up to their knees in blocked drains collapsing under the weight of the monsoon. Typists tapped away under verandahs, churning out elaborate letters dictated by whispering illiterates ejecting bloody mouthfuls of betal nut juice from the ruddle-red corners of rotting mouths. Turning left onto Park street I eventually wound my way onto Sudder Street and a dormitory room in the Paragon Guest House.

Western travellers lounged around green wooden tables, some playing cards, some reading, some doing nothing. I didn't speak other than to enquire about somewhere to sleep and somewhere to wash. After a couple of poached eggs on toast I sat and watched night fall. The occasional peal of laughter began to relax and clean my head of the city's nausea. I climbed the few steps to a small high roofed room where a corner of Calcutta belonged to me for that night.

It was hot and humid and very still; it was sure to rain. The fan spun round, flapping at the night and the gentle sounds of slumber. I was aching to the point where the muscles released involuntary spasms. As I tried to find a more comfortable position on my creaky hessian bed, my heart palpitated and my mind held images that could burst the banks of a river in flood. Staring up to the ceiling, I lay on my back and shook as never before.

At night, the centre of this city was nearly silent. The monsoon-flooded streets had quelled the honking taxis and the tinkling of bicycle rickshaws had been appeased until morning. I woke and slept and then shot bolt upright sweating from the force of a nightmare.

Wednesday morning dawned and a chill shivered me to the quick. The room filled with creaking hessian beds and snorting bags of sleepy humans. I washed, dressed and wandered a couple of street corners to the Blue Sky café. Large glasses of frothy tea cost three rupees and the famous Calcutta banana curd, four and a half. Calcutta was one of two planned rest stops, the other non-cycling day would be in Singapore. Without a little free time, it was possi-

ble my fatigue would build up to a level where it would be hard to recover quickly. Peering out of the window I spied a rickshaw man standing up on the pedals of his bicycle. Flexing yesterday's aching tendons, he too yawned into his day. The flood waters rippled darkly as young boys sloshed about. The rickshaw man rented his vehicle for a couple of rupees from a middleman who may own sixty. His breakfast was a few ounces of rice mixed with some onion and chilli. Tea was at noon and maybe a little curry dish before smoking the dog-end of a well flattened beedi prior to retiring at the end of the day.

As I finished my tea, bald dogs scavenged listlessly only to snatch at chicken heads and assorted flotsom. Bloated and gassy, a kitten bobbed up and down in the monsoon waters – its bones sucked dry by the dogs.

By now it was mid-morning and I had arranged to see an old friend. Major Bennet and his wife lived and worked at the Salvation Army headquarters for East India on the corner of Dharantola Street. It was two years since I had seen them and the Major was more or less as I remembered him. Tired eyes sparkled still whilst his voice was quieter and more resigned to the inevitablilty of all things. His nostalgia for all things British gave him the remote air of someone living in an Imperial past which no longer accorded with the reality of modern India.

'I was just thinking about you,' he said, 'come upstairs and meet Mrs Bennet, she would love to see you.' Lank grey hair fell to one side of his face, above a nose slightly flattened by a good deal of Navy boxing. 'We have considered retiring you know, but back home I'm a fish out of water. I was in London last year and had to ask a newsagent for the price of a first class stamp.' The Colonel, I was to hear he had been promoted, had spent twenty months in Britain these past twenty-six years. 'I pushed my way onto buses and trains and one lady thought I was terribly rude, but that is what we do here.' He broke off from what he was saying to welcome a small plumpish lady who talked incessantly with a Scottish accent quite unhindered by half a life in India.

'Tea and cakes, dear boy,' said Mrs Bennet, 'yer lookin' well considerin'' and we chatted and reminisced about old times.

'Do yer remember when yer came here last time,' she said rummaging about in an old shoe box. 'I call this my memorabilia box, somewhere I've got a photo of yer on that bicycle.' Thrusting a small polaroid picture in front of me, she made me look at myself. 'You've changed boy, my God you've changed.' In the picture I looked happy and secure, completely at ease with the adventure. Now I was ever mindful of the task I'd set myself. I felt fragile and uncertain.

Tradition is very important to people like the Bennets, and when they ran the Sally Army Guest House on Sudder Street, a pot of tea was one rupee, four o'clock on the table on the dot. We ate tea under a portrait of the Queen. Posters of Princess Di and Charles that grace bathroom walls all over Asia, do more than cover up flaking bits of plaster. For the Bennets of this world, monarchy, good manners, pride and regular meal times meant everything.

I didn't drink my tea on account of having stirred in two heaped tablespoonfuls of salt. 'The sugar did look a little funny,' I said to Mrs Bennet afterwards, 'but I didn't like to say.' She had a good laugh and I had to say goodbye. The Colonel made his driver and car available to take me to the airport later in the evening and then said,

'When you come to Calcutta again, you must stay with us, I will take you for a round of golf at the Tollygunge Club. I did 56 holes last Saturday, what do you think of that?'

I jumped into one of Calcutta's armadillo-shaped taxis and sat resplendently. The seats slung so low it was just possible by craning the neck to peer out of the window. Having been soaked for a week in more rain than I had seen in a lifetime, I felt like a knight in shining armour who had just sacrificed his steed. Thoughts of the journey would be pushed as far back into my mind as my energy would allow.

I had promised to meet the Indian publishers Rupa and Co. on Bankim Chatterjee Street and we rattled and honked under the gutters of bits of buildings that occasionally crashed to the pavement.

Old Mr Mehru did not arrive in the office until one o'clock these days, so whilst I waited and sipped coffee supplied by his son, I thumbed through Geoffrey Moorhouse's book, *Calcutta*, which had been squashed on a famous College Street book stall between Lord Curzon's *British Government in India* and Desmond Doigs' *Calcutta; an Artist's Impression.*' I had read Moorhouse before and it was he who instigated my fascination with the city. Statistics for 1963 show that whilst 7,870 people live in every square mile of Los Angeles, and 27,000 in New York, here it is over 102,000. The Reserve Bank of India published a report in 1970 suggesting that if a calorific

instead of financial measurement is used as the baseline of poverty, then 70 per cent of India's people live in poverty. If London has 16 bridges over the Thames to serve a population half a million or so greater than Calcutta, here there is only Howrah Bridge. One quarter of the 600 or so red double-decker buses break down each day trying to carry an average 85 passengers on each journey between dawn and dusk; the average load of a London bus over the same period of time is 17. Yet amid this chaotic bustle, the creative urge and the need to write and to be seen to have something in print has produced more publishers in Calcutta than in the rest of India put together. It's the city of actualist film maker Satyajit Ray, there are more poets here than novelists in Dublin, and as many extravagant gestures in Bengali cinema as any stage theatre in Moscow, Shanghai or anywhere else in the world. Transfixed by this cloying land of charm and decay I

was duly summoned to meet Mr Mehru, head of Rupa Enterprises.

Downstairs from Rupa and Co. was the Indian Coffee House, supposedly famous for the intellectual banter that beat about its smokey walls. It was hardly a house, more like the inside of some grandiose Victorian edifice packed with students sitting under a network of barely rotating nicotine-stained yellow fans. The walls had been covered in one see-through coat of billious-green whitewash, alopecia patches of white still showing through. Perched up in the gods overlooking the stalls, a darkly stained wooden ballustrade fitted tightly around more young people trying to squeeze in. At regular intervals a call of 'bearah' sounded and a wizened old waiter wearing a crusty white tunic cursed and spat and sidled between tables and chairs. On his head he wore a hat which looked as if it had been crossed with a Mohican wig and a braided skirt. Occasionally a flurry of rain fell outside, and inside the talk continued.

During my only really free day on the journey so far, I intended to get as far away from cycling around the world as possible. I didn't want to talk about it and worked hard at not thinking about it, but as I dashed from one old haunt to another, the journey was never too far away from my thoughts. Soon I would have to drive over to the airport and catch my flight to Bangkok. First I should eat.

The curry house was only around the corner but I had to roll up my trousers and wade along roads jammed with the monsoon floods. The street vendors, perched as they were on their shelf-like shops, thought it hugely funny a Westerner having to wade through such slime. Sitting cross-legged and peering at me, they laughed through lips stained crimson with betel nuts and said I should swim to the curry house. I was European and couldn't be anything else. But looking back at Sudder Street the customary number of orange saried head-shaven hippies stood expressionless, until their money ran out, trying to be Indians.

As the sun began to set, the heavily laden sky became patchy and I had found the restaurant for which I'd been looking. The formica-topped tables were stained with the long dusty days. Curling portraits of Howrah Bridge gathered grime against dirty cream walls. The floods had caused an electricity failure and several cobwebby light bulbs hung listlessly in the darkness. My arrival sent a large man in an even larger dhoti scurrying this way then that, as if looking for divine intervention, or at least someone who could lend him a lamp.

I sat down and apart from a group of men chatting to each other by a stone slab doubling as the kitchen table, there was no one else in the restaurant. After ordering spinach, cheese, egg curry and a paratha, and breathing in the acrid smell of burnt chapatis, I leant back waiting for something to happen. Eventually a serving boy carried in an old paraffin lamp and placed it on a table near the far wall where I sat. I closed my eyes. After some time had passed I was aware of a gentle piston-action, slow and rhythmic, cautiously pausing only to begin again, softly then quickly. I looked towards the lamp which was now very close and saw the unshirted youth labouring. A layer of sweat covered a muscular torso which gleamed as he pumped. The pressure in the reservoir vapourised the paraffin and a fine jet of gas shot as high as his head and he smiled. At once he checked the flame, reducing it to fit the capacity of the lamp only to shoot it towards the ceiling again and create his own very peculiar gesture. It was a performance and I was the honoured guest. The more intensely I watched, the more elaborate the ritual became, his sweat and bright teeth reflected the light, straggling black hair clinging to a strong neck as he commanded the attention of the restaurant. The incandescence danced shadows on the wall. It was an art to manipulate the tetchy controls of a creaky paraffin lamp during the monsoon in Calcutta, and once every electricity failure, this boy would be allowed to emerge from behind his cockroach-infested corner to grace us with a few moments of theatrical triumph. My meal arrived along with a chair positioned on top of the table on which the magic lamp was placed. The lamp had been for me.

My flight to Bangkok was due to depart Calcutta at 11 p.m. and at 8 p.m. the Colonel's chauffer-driven car arrived to take me to the airport. I didn't want to leave India because I had not had time to experience more than a tiny fraction of its splendours and its hardships. Wheeling my bike to the checkout desk I was given my boarding pass and then made my way through immigration. On the plane I picked up a magazine, and flicked blankly through its contents. I was tired beyond belief, too tired almost, to sleep. Reclining my seat I rested my head and turning to look out of the window I saw the dark night, sprinkled with the distant lights of Calcutta. The darkness comforted me. Placing my hands over my face I shielded my eyes from the lights of the aircraft's cabin. Desperately seeking comfort, I wished with all my heart that this journey would end.

6 · THE FAR EAST

Bangkok Airport was bright and clean, as safe as any airport I have known. It was 4 a.m. and deciding not to risk any dangers of the night I rolled out my sleeping bag in a hidden corner behind a stack of chairs. Closing my eyes for a couple of hours, I would continue *Day 34* after sunrise. It was still bright when I stirred but the airport lights were softened by a sunny morning. It had been a restful, dreaming sleep and it felt wasteful to wake as I did, in the middle of such colouful images. The bag was warm, cosy even, and collecting my thoughts I looked around. No longer hidden by the stack of chairs I peered through a forest of shoes and legs. The chairs had been distributed around the arrival hall and placed in rows. A packed airport seemed to be waiting for me to waken. Not wanting to disturb me, the chair attendant had wound his seats around me, the rows bulging either side of where I lay. It was a kind gesture and as I climbed out of my bag sheepishly, people nodded politely and smiled. It was 8 a.m. and I had overslept. After stuffing the bag into one of the panniers, I looked around, said goodbye and wheeled my bike out of the airport to join the maelstrom of traffic screaming its way south towards the city of Bangkok.

I'd been to Bangkok a couple of times before and as much as I tried to dislike the place I actually enjoyed the sophisticated clamour. During the journey, I have sometimes wanted to be seen and always I've wanted to hide away; I've wanted to be alone and quiet and then emerge as from some tranquil dream into the noise of the world. Bangkok has 400 *wats* or temple-monasteries, deep inside which you hear only the pacing of bare feet and the murmur of prayer. Outside I crossed the railway line, and Petchburi Road, elbowing my way between lorries and taxis, desperate to be mobile. Crossing Plonchit Road I ended up on one of the main arterial roads out of the city, Rama Four.

The *Bangkok* Post newspaper was on Rama Four, already an hour down on schedule, I decided another hour would not be a serious delay if I called on the paper and kept a long standing appointment with one of its columnists.

George Street was wearing the same maroon-coloured sleeveless sweater that I saw him in a year ago. His trousers, then as now were baggy, and unzipped at the front. With a world-weary miserable expression, he welcomed me, eventually inviting me to sit down. Pinned to an upright filing cabinet, several girlie photographs had been well thumbed. Pulling out a pipe from his

shirt pocket his hands shook as he emptied the tobacco ash into the top drawer of his desk. He smiled, 'New offices you see, they complain if I make a mess on the floor.' A year ago George's hand wrote steadily and even, now I noticed a tremor cross his face followed by a flash of panic. The offices were new, the *Post* was a high technology newspaper, it was all bright cream walls and video display units, everywhere except the corner where George sat. However fresh and sparkling his furniture had been, it was now a sullen, grimy little corner stale with pipe smoke. I imagined myself feeding copy into my word processor, the latest story would be transmitted to the printer in a matter of seconds. Yet I could also be as I imagined George, misplaced and a law unto himself.

Fiddling with his pen he looked at me with a sarcastic grin. 'How long are you staying in town this time, ten minutes?'

'Oh, an hour or so. I only wanted to see if you were still alive,' I said cheekily.

'Ha!' and he laughed, 'and am I?'

'You look great.'

'I feel fine.'

When I shook hands with this tired journalist, he trembled. I had a feeling I wouldn't see him again.

It wasn't necessary to see George except that it gave me some reassurance knowing someone on the other side of the world. Stepping out of the air-conditioned building and into the heaving traffic reminded me of the record. In Europe I was nearly a day behind schedule, now it was one and half hours. If I was to reach Singapore as planned, it was vital I didn't lose too much time now.

Two hours after leaving the paper I was cycling west to Nakhon Pathom on a road bordered by rice paddies, their stalks blowing in the wind. A little further on, the wind dropped and the reflection of an occasional tree could be

seen in the still waters. Further into the afternoon the grey sky had become blue. For some reason I had forgotten to buy a map of Thailand, but in my diary I had already made a list of the major towns I would have to cycle through.

Day 34: The route through Thailand to Malaysia
Day 35: Bangkok – Hua Hin – Prachuap Khiri Khan.
Day 36: Prachuap – Chumphon – Surat Thani.
Day 37: Surat Thani – Phatthalung – Songkhla – Hat Yai.

All morning I rode fast, the route was flat and the wind was blowing me south. There were 1,450 miles between me and Singapore and just seven days to get there. With over 5,500 miles completed since the start of the journey and nearly 15,000 miles since January I was confident I could now ride at least 200 miles a day. A serious delay at this stage could destroy my chances of cycling around the world under that magic 80 days. All my flights were staggered according to my schedule of 170 miles each day, to miss one flight could cause delays of several days, maybe weeks.

Past villages with names I had no ability to pronounce, I stayed on the road to Singapore. I cycled into late afternoon as the sun began to set. It was quite dark and only when the moon began to rise could I see the road clearly. There was no traffic, just the plaintive cries of children being scolded, or families sitting down to eat. After 190 miles into *Day 34*, in the darkness, in Thailand, I wasn't afraid, but I was alone. For me the day was 14 hours' old, another hour or so would be enough cycling. Tomorrow it would start all over again.

Laying out my sleeping bag between the road and a group of ragged bushes, I sat down to eat a little chocolate and

bread. My diet had become very simple, I didn't know how sustaining the food was but I felt strong. The moon looked bulbous and heavy and hovering over some stretch of water its edges wobbled. The moon was hallucinating. So was I. It was all too much to understand, each day being so far removed from the everyday person within me. As I sat munching my bread I remembered the last time I was in Bangkok, the first time I'd biked around the world. I tried hard to understand the nature of certain things, the meaning of comfort in a faraway land. I could have got drunk, but then I'd fall over and remember nothing. I could have taken any drug I'd ever heard of, but I had a feeling it would scramble my mind. It could have been sought in prayer, but I was never sure of its effectiveness. I

might have considered sleeping with a woman, but I wasn't sure if I could spare the money. Wandering into a decrepit café near the Malaysia Hotel, I sat down and ordered a Coke. Noticing a woman looking at me I smiled, I wasn't entirely sure of the proceedure but it seemed a reasonable start. She smiled back immediately, beautiful white teeth except for two that were gold. I remembered my heart beating the same way I first made love. It had been several weeks of yearning before the time was right, two days after my last exam, forty minutes before leaving to live in France. Her zip had jammed and I had to prise off her trousers with a pair of pliers. I smiled at the memory and as I looked up, another girl smiled back. 'You like her Mister, she very good girl, are you very good boy?' I felt

awful. What ever might happen didn't seem right, but neither was it entirely wrong. I murmured something about her being very nice and smiled again. I remember biting my lip for being so stupid, this was an occasion demanding care and discretion and all I could do was smile like a moron. 'She not expensive, you want, I will act for her, she can be your girlfriend, how much you pay?' I didn't know the going rate off hand so I let her suggest a price. She said 500 bahts, about £12, and slightly ashamed I said 400 and she said yes. The money was paid in advance, and we were shown our room.

Prostitution is common in Bangkok and what felt like a poignant occasion, probably occured several times each minute every night, including weekends and bank holidays. There was something nagging at my thoughts. The degrading circumstances in which I was to perform a potentially beautiful act made me feel very sad. I now understood that a journey around the world is less to do with the beautiful things, rather it makes you examine yourself in the light of ugly experiences. I closed the door behind me. The room was bare except for a bed that sagged in the middle, a wash basin by the one small window, and a toilet that looked quite unlike a white water lily; it looked like what it was, the enlarged end of a sewer pipe. I wasn't smiling now, I had made a commitment to myself. She was undressing, first her blouse, then her crumpled sarong fell to the floor. I remember thinking how different this woman's body might be, servicing the needs of so many men. When she was clothed I could imagine more or less what she looked like naked, but between the approximation of the idea and the precision of reality there was a small gap of the unimaginable, and it was this breach that proved exciting. In a hurried glance her body looked pleasant enough, large brown breasts strapped in a slightly grubby bra, strong thighs holding up a stomach that had stretched from having carried too many babies too soon.

I was wearing a tie, which I always do when going for a drink, as I wasn't drinking I decided to take it off. She lay on the bed laughing. It was becoming a farce and I was doing quite well in the lead role. I felt utterly useless on three counts: I wanted to talk but didn't speak Thai and she understood little English, I couldn't undo my shirt buttons, and the third little detail we hadn't reached yet. I wished for a moment I'd prayed or better still got drunk. After a few moments I stood naked by the window. The café light from the downstairs entrance flickered, lighting me eerily as in a bad dream. All of a sudden I had an erection, and that was strange, because I hadn't been thinking of the girl but the flickering light. A friend once told me that during *any* kind of dream men have erections, which suggests that the link between erections and naked women is one of a thousand ways such clockwork can be started in a man's head. How vile. Had my seeing so much of the world made me oblivious to the feelings of another human being? I felt depressed.

No longer supported, her breasts lay to each side of her body, quite still, I couldn't even detect a heartbeat, I wasn't entirely sure she was awake. Some women I have known have guarded their nakedness apprehensively, as though trying to express the

value of their body by the modesty given to it. This girl had broken with such modesty. She had only one other choice; to labour all day in the sun, bent double in the rice paddies for a pittance of what she could earn on her back. She could hardly be blamed. Had we been

able to converse I daresay she would have asserted that beauty and youth were worthless and overrated. As I lay next to her, her very ordinary face had no glow at all and I felt sorry for her. If she had been pretty she could have asked for twice what I'd paid. Her breasts were soft, and they were shaped in the way honey settles having immediately fallen from a spoon.

Opening her eyes she said she wanted me and by that time I suppose I wanted her, but to continue would be to exploit her. If only I could have been satisfied by that flickering light, I need not have disturbed myself or her with the aggressive stupidity of sex. As I lay on top of her I didn't know whether I was acting from a point of strength, trying to exorcize some hidden fear and loathing by confronting myself with this particular degradation; or was I seeking the least way of human resistance by submitting to a natural desire? I didn't know the

answer. I was simply sad, for her and for me.

I started as the whole night lit up. A lorry drove past, its headlights shining in my face. Looking at my watch I saw it was past midnight, I'd been thinking about Bangkok for over an hour and had to be on the road in four hours. A wind was drifting across the paddies, warm and moist, at least the mosquitos would be kept away. I closed my eyes and slept deeply.

The next day, *Day 35*, started at 4.30 a.m. and ended at midnight. Resting only an hour and a half I rode 230 miles in 18 hours, an average speed of nearly 13 miles per hour. My diary entry for the day recorded where I'd begun today and where it had ended; Prachuap to Surat Thani. It had also recorded the words '*too tired to write.*' I was exhausted. After four hours sleep I continued into *Day 36* towards the Thai-

81

Malaysian border. The rice paddies were fewer, replaced by rubber trees and plantations that cast the road in a shadow as soon as the sun began to set. I was numbed by the adventure, tired beyond belief and alternately angry and ecstatic. I had badly underestimated this section of the journey, my laid back attitude to planning was unforgivable. The joints in my knees began to bleed. The edges of my knees were swollen and in the middle of the knee-cap, a dark band of blood blackened by the hour. Bruises appeared on my thighs, blood was obviously suppurating from muscle fibres that had been torn by the effort. As I crossed the border during the morning of *Day 37* my nose began to bleed and it wouldn't stop. All morning I cycled and still it bled. Blocking my nose with tissue stemmed the flow only as long as it took the blood to find my throat. From that moment I felt sick.

Day 37: From Thailand into Malaysia. I am ill

Where am I? It all hurts. It isn't just the cycling. Waves of nausea hit me and I feel the journey no longer has any worth. Sitting next to me by a bag of rubbish, a little boy rocks back on his heels, to and fro. A crow perches on top of the rubbish scavaging debris. Another bag is flung at the feet of the crow. The little boy looks at me bewildered. I couldn't decide whether it was because of me that he was upset or because he had to share the same space with the rubbish and the crow.

The roads in Malaysia accommodated more traffic than in Thailand and were in a poorer condition. I had to be in Singapore by the evening of *Day 40*

catch my overnight flight to Perth. I would have to continue cycling on *Day 41* to Merridin and there would be little respite until my next day off in Sydney. I desperately needed a day's rest so I decided to try to reach Singapore half a day earlier. By increasing my average speed from 12 to 14 miles per hour over the three days in Malaysia I would gain around 90 miles. Cycling hard from early morning to early morning I raced as never before through the jungle. Resting only to eat and drink I rode furiously. Names flashed by; Butterworth, Ipoh, Kuala Lumpur, Melaka. In the heat and humidity the days were sickly and between food stops I went along as fast as I was able for as long as possible. On and on I cycled, with hardly time to think and even less energy to spare. The bruises on my legs were still there but my nose bleed had clotted. For two days I breathed only through my mouth. I was getting closer

and closer and within sight of the end of Peninsular Malaysia, I was determined to have my free day. *Day 37* came and went as did *Day 38* and with the greatest of effort so did *Day 39*. At last, in a pitch dark, windless night, I arrived at the most southerly city in Malaysia, Johor Bahru, and approached the Malayasian-Singapore border. Towards the end of *Day 39* I was marginally up on schedule and that would afford me a day's rest in the Singapore Hilton. At the very end of *Day 39* I checked into the hotel and collapsed on the bed, unwashed and fully clothed. Only then did I begin to understand what it meant to try to do something completely original, but how could I have known it was going to be so hard? The headlights of cars pierced the darkness behind my closed eyes, and my ears drummed with the sound of rattling trucks. My whole body shook involuntarily, maybe the spasms continued as I slept, I had no more energy to control them.

There was a knock on the door. The hotel porter had brought me a bouquet of flowers, a basket of fruit, and a very hot cup of tea. As he arranged the flowers carefully on a table by the television, I was about to thank him, when I realised I was still dressed and covered in the grime of nearly three days cycling. Still stiff and sore I was about to apologise, but he said it wasn't necessary and informed me that the Front Desk Manageress was waiting for me in the breakfast room and that I was invited to join her. In less time than it took to drink the tea, I had showered, dressed in my spare set of clothes and went to speak to the Manageress.

Having heard of my early arrival, a press conference had been arranged later that morning in the hotel. Two Chinese papers would be there, *The Straits Times*, Singapore's leading newspaper, Singapore television and radio, and a gentleman from the news agency Reuters. There was an hour to go and having just eaten six boiled eggs I wondered if I could eat a seventh. Having eaten so much tropical fruit, I was beginning to feel the warning signs of a rumbling stomach. It was safer my eating eggs. Any more mangos or papayas and I'd be spending more time crouching behind a bush than on the bike.

Singapore is quite a good stopover for round the world travellers before journeying on to either Indonesia or South East Asia. Later that evening I would board a flight to Perth, arriving in the early morning.

According to my maps and diary I had ridden nearly 7,000 miles since leaving home, and that was less than six weeks ago. It felt like half a lifetime. Singapore was seven hours ahead of home so at midday I had to phone various radio stations in Britain to chat on their breakfast shows. During the afternoon, more press arrived and I phoned my local radio stations and newspapers to say how I was progressing and all the journalists here signed my diary again to validate my journey. As I approached the other side of the world I was dully aware that friends, relatives and business associates were existing quite well without me. I put thoughts of home into a little locked box in my mind, marked 'not to be opened until *Day 79*'.

7 · AUSTRALIA

Checking into my Perth hotel room at 2 a.m. I was then sick until daybreak. Recognising the symptoms from a previous journey, I knew I'd contracted gardia, a bowel parasite which was very debilitating and difficult to destroy completely. Without treatment, the weakening effect of the disease would drag me down to the side of the road and in parts of Australia that is the same as being left to die.

Day 41: Sickness in Perth
Lying in bed looking out of the window, I am smiling. The journey is halfway over, and I only have to cycle across Australia and America. I laugh at such a crazy thought. Now I feel better after being ill all night and this first day in Australia seems so bright and new. Now the journey has a better chance of succeeding. Communications and emergency services exist and speaking English helps! A ferry sails from one side of an inlet to another and she is coloured gold by the sun. I haven't seen the sun for three weeks, and then it was only a reflected glimpse in the back window of a Bombay taxi.

After I had eaten a lovely breakfast, a Western Australian news team came to film my leaving Perth. I threw up over somebody's front lawn but was only saved from disgracing myself on cam-era by a sycamore tree being in the way. That was the signal to see the doctor. After prescribing Flagyel, tablets designed to obliterate all known bugs in the bowel, he then suggested I not ride my bike for a week. If I accepted his advice I would be 1,700 miles down on schedule.

I liked Perth. Never before having been to Australia, I had no idea how the east coast would differ from this peaceful and pretty part in the west. Having vomited for the first five hours of my six-hour stay in Perth, it was nearly impossible to have any ideas whatsoever.

The crossing of Australia was going to be physically hard but at least I didn't have the bureaucratic problems of Jordan and India. The frontier attitude of Australians made them sympathetic to mad escapades. When I applied for my visa at the Australian Consulate, they told me to collect it in ten days. On hearing about my proposed bicycle crossing of Australia, they returned my passport fully stamped in ten minutes.

By late afternoon I'd cycled 100 miles, and two hours into the evening had completed another 50. Now dark and cold, I approached the outskirts of the town of Merredin. A late-night garage sold hamburgers and coffee and in this way I consumed dinner in ten minutes: my second meal-stop in twelve hours. Before rolling out my sleeping bag I had promised to phone Manchester Piccadilly Radio for a live interview. Here, telephone communication was no longer a problem. An old friend, Tim Grundy, asked me to describe the view from the telephone box. In the miserable cold of this Australian night I could hear the familiar noises of Manchester at lunch time. Here, all was black and the light in the box obscured my vision. We chatted for a while and I promised to call twice a week until the end of the journey. Placing the receiver on its hook I was just about to leave the box, when peering through the window I saw a square of light shining from a house. A curtain had been drawn back to display the inside of a living room. The shape of somebody rose as if to stand up, and walking towards the window it shielded its eyes and peered out at me. In several small houses with corrugated roofs other curtains were pulled back. The people in this neatly kept avenue seemed curious about me. Pedalling a few hundred yards around the corner, I rolled out my bag and slept.

It was such a pleasure to cycle in the sun but what suprised me more than anything was the temperature. Dawn was about 7 a.m. and before the sun emerged over the crest of the horizon, freezing mists scattered the cold black road. It never occurred to me that the land where Christmas dinner was eaten whilst sunbathing on the beach could possibly ever be cold. Fifty miles further on I freewheeled into Southern Cross, a town no bigger than a main street. Having spent two days supply of money on my prescription in Perth, I couldn't afford new clothes so hunted around for a second-hand shop. A man selling hot pies directed me along the main street.

'You wanna go see Mrs Hatch, we sell all our junk to her,' he said laughing, 'you'll need to keep warm where you're going.'

I thanked him and rode half-way down the street looking out for the shop. Inscribed on a small sign above a dirty red door were the words, 'Mrs Hatch's Anglican Second-hand Clothes Shop. May the Lord be in Your Soul.' An old lady stepped from out of the back of the shop wearing grey clothes. Below her grey hair, her grey face covered in tight wrinkles frowned suspiciously.

'What do you want?' she demanded.

'Anything to keep me a bit warmer, I've heard the Nullarbor Desert can be cold at night.'

'Well you've heard right ain't yer? Any case, a weedy little shrimp like you ain't expectin' to get far is yer?'

'Well I've managed to get here...'

'Well the desert is special in't it?' She interrupted, 'and if you take my advice turn round and go back.' Her anger unnerved me, I had planned the entire journey around the Nullarbor, ensuring I crossed it in winter.

Paying a couple of pounds for two pairs of tracksuit bottoms, a jumper, a hat and a some woolly socks that doubled as gloves, I felt better prepared. I said goodbye but she shuffled into a back room. As she opened the door I heard the sound of a girl sobbing. As she closed the door behind her, the shop was silent once more. Pulling the socks over my hands I stepped out into the street.

Climbing back onto my bike I rode back up the main street and headed in a slightly north-easterly direction for Coolgardie and then Kalgoorlie. The huge under-belly of a long snaking water pipe gleamed a dull silver in the sun. In the near distance, quartz crystal glinted at me only to become less magical as the reflection of the sun angled elsewhere. Sandy gullies led into the bush, ready to drain away those sudden bursts of rain which appear in the wake of a rare water-soaked night.

Coolgardie was 100 miles away from Southern Cross and it would take me six hours to get there. The road was long and barren. Petrol and food could be bought at roadhouses. Two hours away from Southern Cross I stopped at the first one I'd seen that morning. Near Coca-Cola signs nailed to sun-dried timbers, goats plodded between shelves of food, nibbling at the biscuits. Sipping a coffee, I watched a chicken perch on the back of a chair on the other side of my table. Gobbles of regurgitated corn, white and acrid-smelling, hung stickily from chair to floor. Outside, the sun was as warm as an English summer's day and here I was in the middle of an Australian winter.

By mid-afternoon I rode into Coolgardie. I had a feeling that the further into the fringe of the interior I progressed, the more self-sufficient these townships would become. Coolgardie is large on the Australian map. At the end of the last century it was a bustling city of some 28,000 miners digging out 1,000 tons of pure gold. Now the mines are closed, the gold is hard to get or gone, and in the early seventies only 600 people remained. Eighteen miles further on, Kalgoorlie and its satellite city, Boulder, fared a little better. Being the second city in all of Western Australia's million square miles, the famous 'Golden Mile' main street would have seen more than 200,000 prospectors gambling and drinking their nights away with hard liquor and easy women.

Today I had ridden nearly 200 miles in 13 hours. There were few indicators of exact mileage in such vastness, but it wasn't difficult to cycle 15 miles per hour if the wind was blowing favourably. I knew from years of riding that if I rotated the pedals approximately 70 times every minute using a gearing of 52 teeth on the front chainwheel with the chain wrapped around the 18-toothed back sprocket, I would ride one mile in four minutes. From sunrise to sunset, the wind blew strongly from the west and every morning until the end of the journey I woke up and knew by the direction of my rustling hair, whether or not I could still break the world record. There were lots of other elements that affected the outcome of the journey such as customs, accidents, stomach bugs, and injuries, but a strong headwind would force me to ride at half my usual speed.

Sitting in the small Majestic café on Hannan Street in the centre of Kalgoorlie, I ate a good portion of pie and chips washed down with a mug of coffee. My state of fitness had reached a level I thought unattainable. Cycling 100 miles no longer seemed very far and as long as I wasn't struggling into a headwind I was hardly out of breath. Using my body so intensely, I became more aware of its functions. My heartbeat was firm and steady, rising only when the level of effort had to be temporarily raised. My leg muscles were lean, stringy almost, the fat having long since been burnt off. The skin was brown now, protecting me from the mild winter sun. I became like an animal sitting on its haunches, nervous, waiting to sprint away.

Looking out of a window masked with the lettering of some cigarette advert, I gazed across the street where timber-built buildings resembled the

Wild West frontage of a Hollywood film set. I imagined such buildings to be supported by wooden verandahs from the front and hidden struts from behind.

Progress had been so good today that I stepped out of the cafe with the view of indulging myself with a tour of the town. I got little further than the bike when a fellow from a parked van shouted over and welcomed me.

'What are you doing?'

I told him I'd ridden from Perth and that I was on my way to Sydney.

'You think you're being hard done by, the old prospectors used to push wheelbarrows from Perth to Kalgoorlie looking for gold. Anyway, the name's Bob, I'm off to the "Two-Ups," penny-tossing, do you want to come along?'

Journeying has taught me an acute sense of character and awareness of safety. The eyes tell all. If they remain wide and open they appear honest and sincere. If they narrow and fail to look at me long and hard, they represent someone who cannot be trusted. This fellow's eyes were open and steady so I loaded the bike in the back of his van.

Motoring along a well-used dirt track which wound around the scrappiest of bush, outcrops of limestone melted to the magna below. Bob was a builder renovating a nearby motel and afterwards we would eat with his mates in the restaurant. Presently, I spotted a round hut in the distance, and before long heard the excited cries of a game in session. Some standing some seated, and with the exception of two women, all were men and all seemed to take the game very seriously. Their eyes concentrated on two pennies being tossed into the air, and as the pennies abruptly fell somewhere in the sandy ring encircled by the audience, the silence was audible.

'Heads and tails' shouted the 'Two-Up' penny-tosser's assistant, and a large man with arms covered in tatoos collected outstanding payments and doled out winnings as the need was due. The house was in uproar until the next throw was signalled.

'Aussies in Europe give us a bad name,' Bob said, 'they're the "hocker-type," all beer and birds, that's not all we think about you know.' He paused. 'We also like the betting,' and he threw ten dollars to the collector.

In this rough mining crowd, I was obviously not Australian and I wondered how many here were representative of Australia. Treated with the cordial respect and indifference bestowed on strangers, I sat and revelled in a brand new experience. Occasionally I glimpsed the scrambled features of a pick-axe beaten face staring at me from across the circle. My features were finer, less manly, boyish almost and I must have looked quite incongruous. All I could do to reassure myself was to consider that cycling around the world and averaging 171 miles a day was a severe test for any man, however boyish I appeared.

'Yaw, I've seen the world. Me, you know, on the seas. In the Navy of course. The conditions were bad then.' An old fellow began speaking to me in a way which allowed for no pause until he drew breath. 'I can talk with everyone in the world because I've seen it, yer see.' He sniffed, paused as if to sneeze then made the most horrendous noise through his nose. He said he had a cold but the snorting had the rhythm of a mental disorder. 'That's why I look so young,' he said, and as the pennies clinked and the crowd hung white-knuckled to their seats, I looked at this old man who couldn't bring himself to look at me. His raincoat was open to reveal a holed woolly cardigan showing a tea-stained cream shirt tucked into wide flared trousers.

I didn't think travelling had made me look any younger. The years of being on the road were beginning to take their toll. Wrinkles were beginning to form on my own face and they would dig deep.

'Naw, naw I had a problem with me. You know I couldn't piddle so the doctors had a fiddle until I could do it,' he added whilst looking at the ground.

I was led to believe Australia was a land of characters. The 'Two-Ups' continued to clink and the old man continued to snort, now sounding like a camel. 'The quacks said I looked as if I could do with a bit of new blood having lost a bit so they gave me two pints.' He took a deep breath, 'suppose it was young blood and that rejuvenates you and that's why I don't look seventy-eight years old.' He certainly didn't look that old, and turning away he muttered something about having to lay down a dollar and disappeared into the crowd.

Bob was keen to return, not having won anything, and half an hour later we were back in the dark outskirts of town. Bob drove me along the road in the red-light district where a row of corrugated huts sheltered the girls and their clients. 'They dragged one of the Shelias off last week with AIDS,' Bob said, 'half the population of the town are as white as a sheet, they've probably seen their own ghost,' and he laughed. Seated on their bed, puposefully parked by a well lit doorway, the girls cavorted mechanically whenever a car drove past. A fat man sidled into one of the doorways and after a moment's discussion the door was closed.

Bob drove me back to the hotel he was staying in and let me use the shower in his room. Enjoying the hot water on my body I wondered when I would have the chance to shower again. I felt good. The journey was halfway over and I was still on schedule. Laughing quietly to myself, nothing could stop me now, I thought, and I laughed louder. Suddenly a pain stabbed the side of my chest. I flung my arms around the pain, clutching my chest. My face creased with the agony. The water was burning my back but I couldn't move. It wasn't my heart, but then I wasn't sure. It was my kidneys. I moved towards the shower curtain. About to collapse I lunged forward grabbing at the taps, a towel rail, the curtain. My thoughts went white and the floor of the shower was now red. Kneeling in the shower I then fell over onto my shoulder and the pain near my stomach shot to my chest. I lay on the floor terrified. Was this a heart attack? I tried to get up and standing for a moment, fell to my knees again. Easing my way out of the shower and with my face pressed against the carpet of Bob's bedroom floor, I vomited. I was sicker than I'd ever been in my life. This journey was a cursed wretched adventure. At that moment Bob walked in and as far as I could remember threw a towel over me and with a little difficulty picked me up and, shouting for one his labourers to help, they carried me to Bob's car. The journey to the hospital was a nightmare. On the way I was sick twice. I tried to apologise, but everytime I opened my mouth something came out.

I was so terribly embarrassed. If only I had known that this was going to happen, I would have gone into the desert to be alone. Again I was sick on entering the reception room, I couldn't believe what was happening. The pain was excruciating. The thought that I wasn't strong enough to complete a journey which was now a burning obsession was more than I could bear. On the bike I felt fine, for the last 42 days I felt fine, for the last 6,500 I had suffered from nothing more serious than exhaustion. My mental attitude to this journey was strong and uncompromising, but I was beginning to consider for the first time the breakdown of my body. Immediately I was placed on a stretcher and taken into the examination room. I made a mental note for my diary.

Day 42: Kalgoorlie Hospital on the edge of the Nullarbor Plain
I'm shivering and cold and still so far away from home. I want to be home more than anything else in the world. The excitement of the journey has been replaced by a marathon of determination and stamina of which I have only a little left.

The night nurse told me to wait for the doctor, he was on his way. I felt less vulnerable now but didn't feel any better. After a while the doctor arrived and asking me to lie down, examined me. After hearing I'd been to Africa, particularly Egypt so recently, he began looking for bilharzia, a parasite that is part of the life cycle in snails which penetrates skin in water. Blood in the urine would indicate a bleeding bladder. A little blood was detected but even that could be accounted for by muscular fatigue. The risk of malaria was high in some of the countries I'd passed through, notably India and parts of Thailand. I didn't have a fever but my thyroid gland was swollen and I was becoming disorientated. As he peered into my eyes, I laid back and wondered if it were possible to sleep with a torch searching through a bloodshot iris. I was desperately tired. Next

the doctor asked for a sample of urine and gave me a plastic box in which to deposit a stool. He would test for dysentery of which he said there were two types, amoebic and bacillary. Both show mucus and blood-stained diarrhoea and fortunately mild cases while common, would not necessarily halt the journey. The results from this test would be known in a few days and if I were to reach Adelaide, which was about 1,300 miles away, I was to ring him for the details. The doctor said my spleen was badly swollen but that could simply be a matter of having slept on the side of a cold road for most of the last forty-two days. He said that I was to be very careful for the next few days, but he didn't say the journey need terminate, he knew such advice would be ignored.

Doctor Rob, as I was to know him, was the gentlest of men and the staff at the hospital the most courteous I'd known. I'd been in Australia for two days and I couldn't have been made more welcome. He wanted me to stay overnight but I insisted I return to my belongings. Armed with tablets, vitamins and several prescriptions, I bade him goodbye, eased myself into a taxi and at three o'clock in the morning climbed into bed. If I was to complete tomorrow's schedule I would have to be on the road by sunrise.

It was something of an understatement to say it wasn't easy getting out of bed on *Day 43*. Strangely, my illness was not so apparent whilst I cycled. The awareness of the problem lessened as attention was more appropriately directed to riding 171 miles. After that, fatigue usually made rotational movement difficult, and with badly cramped legs, I occasionally fell off.

The air was cold but I was warm and any feeling of discomfort disappeared as the day grew brighter. Some days began with my knowing exactly where I was going and what might be found there, other days I had no idea what might happen. Apart from my temporarily heading south, towards Norseman, I had no idea what lay just this side of sunset. My map showed telephone boxes, which, strung across the desolate Nullarbor Plain, were between 70 and 100 miles apart. Settlements along this lonely road were no more than the roadhouses and they looked after the telephone boxes. To step off the road and face south was to imagine several thousand miles of South Pacific Ocean and quite a lot of Antarctica. Standing on my pedals on the crest of a small rise, I looked north and pretended I could feel the grit of the Great Victoria Desert and the sweaty heat of the tropical Rum Jungle, 2,000 miles away near Darwin. So as the sun rose, and brand new morning clouds scattered to show an ice-blue sky, I pedalled on without a word, hour after hour, with just the occasional passing truck for company.

At mid-day, the watery winter sun was warm and on the horizon there was the stirring of a haze. As the sun set, the scrub began to resemble a painted photograph. Sepia sand-tracks coloured by jungle-green were startled by splashes of saltbush, blue-bush, occasional mulga, ti trees and sandlewood. Less than 20 miles away from Norseman I'd already cycled 140 miles. Finishing off the remains of a bar of chocolate, I drank the last few drops of milk that had been safely packed away in my panniers all day. Cold milk numbed my mouth and cooled my stomach. About to complete yet another day, I heard a car pull up behind me and a man asked me if I needed any assistance. I didn't, but for

a moment we chatted as he and a lady companion got out to stretch their legs. Standing together, nervously holding hands, they looked at me with awe and pity. It wasn't that he was a small man, rather she was such a size as to necessitate climbing gear and crampons. As she stood, gawping, the top of his head reached the level of motherly breasts which hung, huge and ponderously. They were in love, they said so. As they looked respectively up and down at each other, I noticed the back of their car was sprayed with those immortal words, 'Just Married'.

Further down the road I spotted a hitch-hiker and stopping for a quick chat, shared an orange with him. As long as the record schedule had been maintained, the end of a day was calm and precious. The hitch-hiker was ill-kempt, down and out on the way to Perth. He had been working for a government-run cooperative of young unemployed people.

'Bloody girlfriend's pregnant so I'm off,' he explained.

As the day slowed down to a standstill, I had a little time to talk. 'What are yer carryin'?' he asked, his eyes wandered over every part of my bike, making particular note of my panniers. 'Yer couldn't lend me some money, I'm plum broke, give it yer back when I next see yer.' He was just a bum scrounging his way around a lot of dusty Australian miles. A white minibus drove past, and the driver leaned out of the window and said if I wanted a bed for the night I was to follow them. To rest with young people and soak in the conversation of good times and idle chatter seemed like a good idea. I cycled behind them along a dirt-track to a few cheaply built buildings until we reached their common room where they relaxed and ate.

A wood-burning stove crackled warmly. Ten young people sat around a long wooden table, eating and laughing and stretched out on a sofa. They offered me some coffee and I joined them, gazing through the open door of the stove. The flames made the surrounding air waver.

Sitting in front of a pile of crackling flames, I must have fallen asleep. Suddenly I awoke with a jolt.

'Hope you don't mind,' said one of the lads, 'it's so hot,' and after he pushed back the hatch, I was sitting once again in front of the stove.

Considering the day, I had ridden just over 100 miles. Last night's fever in Kalgoorlie Hospital had abated but I didn't feel well enough to ride further. Comfortably tired, the thought of what was to come made me shudder. If I was to reach Port Augusta by the end of *Day 47*, I would have to ride 1,000 miles in four days. Forcing the pace now, whilst the wind was blowing from the west, would give me a fighting chance to keep on schedule when turning due south along the Spencer Gulf where I knew the winds would cut across me. It was a gamble because I stood the chance of relying too heavily on the wind to cover too much distance too soon. Heavily weighted against this plan was the possibility of only being able to ride 100 miles or so a day whenever the wind should blow against me.

With such a workload for me and the bike, I idly tinkered with what I thought needed repairing. The ballbearings in both wheel hubs sounded smooth, as did the bearings in the front fork head-set, and the bottom-bracket where the chain-wheel spindle passed through the base of the frame. The spokes were taut and, apart from a little wobble, the wheels were as strong now as on the first day. The brake cables hadn't frayed and the chain and rear sprockets seemed to be in good working order. Disliking intensely anything to do with repairing bicycles, I would never have considered myself an ideal candidate for the job of cycling around the world. So I tinkered around, checking all the nuts and bolts, listening for the sounds of a broken machine. I was moments away from sleep, but remembered so clearly my Dad toiling away at my first bike. All evening he laboured over a mechanical problem I didn't understand, and nervously I stood beside him holding my breath. As a child I believed he could do anything, especially if he fixed my bike. Now I was too tired to continue, I just hoped that by morning everything would be alright.

After a good night's sleep I set off early the following morning. The road to Norseman was south and undulating. The wind was blustery and it was difficult to ascertain in which direction I would eventually be pushed. Before reaching the town centre, I turned left to head east. Still the wind panted from all sides and the threat of a headwind made me gasp. There are so many factors governing a bicycle ride around the world: the route climbs or descends, the surface is hard or loose, the sun soothes or burns and the rain exhilarates and freshens, only to move the muscles into a bloody and bruised fatigue at the end of the day. These are all factors to do with the body but there are also the factors of the mind. Today is *Day 44* and the journey will eek its way into the Eucla Basin of the Nullarbor Plain. I was slightly afraid of the Nullarbor, its desolation would accept no compromise, the determination to cross 600 miles of barren landscape has got to be total.

Of the greatest inland explorers of

Australia, I remember reading about Ernest Giles and Charles Stuart, one went into the Western Desert and one stayed out. Stuart nearly died in his brave but tragic and unsuccessful attempt to cross the small and terrible Simpson Desert. Giles had failed to cross it in 1874, turning back when his companion Gibson died, but in 1875 tried it again on a southern route traversing 2,500 miles across the inland edge of the Nullarbor Plain. As he recorded in his journal:

'I represented that we were probably in the worst desert upon the face of the earth, but that fact should give us all the more pleasure in conquering it. We were surrounded on all sides by dense scrubs, and the sooner we forced our way out of them the better. It was of course a desperate thing to do, and I believe very few people would or could rush madly into a totally unknown wilderness, where the nearest known water was 650 miles away. But I had sworn to go to Perth or die in the attempt, and I inspired the whole of my party with enthusiasm. One and all declared that they would live or die with me.'

At the 190-mile point his Afghan camel driver, Salah said: 'Mister Gile, when you get water?' Giles replied, unconcerned, 'Water? pooh! there's no water in this country, Salah. I didn't come here to find water, I came here to die, and you said you'd come and die, too.' Salah persisted, 'I think some camel he die tomorrow, Mr. Gile.'

'No, Salah,' corrected Giles, 'they cannot possibly live till tomorrow. I think they will all die tonight.'

'Oh, Mr. Gile, I think we all die soon now.'

'Oh, yes, Salah, we'll all be dead in a day or two.'

I was on the southernmost edge of this human wasteland, but there were four important differences between my crossing and that of Giles. Now there was a road across the Plain, and every hundred miles or so there was a supply of water. As I rode on towards Balladonia, huge trucks passed me every hour, so should I fall ill, I would almost certainly not be left to die. At least as important as not being alone was the decision I made to cross here in the Australian winter. The whole journey was built around the relatively easier crossing of the Nullarbor Plain when the early morning mists would freeze the sweat of my body only to make way for a warm winter's day. A summer's day in the Nullarbor is as hot and deadly now as it was when Giles walked to Perth.

The edge of the Nullarbor Plain differs in the smallest of ways from that which has gone before. At first, thirsty looking trees are more sparsely scattered and clumps of semi-arid scrub become more prolific, edging themselves along the side of the road and beyond for hundreds of miles. Skirting along the dusty road until noontime, I had ridden at around 17 miles per hour for seven hours and was nearing Balladonia. I imagined all the stops across the Nullarbor to be like Balladonia, little more than a roadhouse where I'd be able to eat, drink and sit down for an hour. By one o'clock I was back on the road again to ride until it was dark. The wind wasn't strong but the slight blowing that came from the stillness encouraged me instead of slowing me down. My legs curved around the bike, following the course of the pedals to carve our way across Australia. Sometimes I imagined different actions of the body to be quite independent of each other. For the most part of the day I had no awareness of my turning legs and such was the rhythm, could feel no pain.

Night had fallen on *Day 44* and I'd ridden 240 miles in 15 hours. I was exhausted. It had been a desperately hard day for which my only reward was a body on the verge of collapse.

Under a brilliantly starlit night I laid out my sleeping bag. Climbing into the warmth, desperate in my tiredness, I had a few moments when my thoughts did not have to be shared with the clod-hopping mechanical process of rotating legs. The Nullarbor was cold now and the road quiet, all I could hear was my unwrapping of a bag of dried fruit and the subsequent squelching of an apricot. Perhaps ten trucks had passed me all day and apart from ordering food at Balladonia, and buying some milk and chocolate for later, nothing had happened. There were times when cycling around the world faster than it may ever be cycled around again was so important to me that it mattered more than life itself. And other days when breaking the record was much less important than simply enjoying the sound of the wind rushing through my hair.

Munching a handful of dates, I looked up at the stars and blinked my way from Hercules to Sagittarius and on again to Pegasus. In less than a breath I had journeyed a third of the whole known southern hemisphere.

The following morning I started riding before the sun had begun to rise. Swirling mists bit the parts of my face that stuck out into the wind, so I pedalled furiously to keep warm. As the sun appeared over the horizon life was beginning to be quite cheerful, and trundling along at a brisk pace, I ate the last of my fruit. The Mundrabilla roadhouse was less than 100 miles away and the chocolate and milk in my panniers would certainly get me there.

After a couple of hours, I suddenly began to sense a loosening of one of my pedal cranks. Within a mile or so the crank was definitely loose so I stopped and placed the bike on its side. The spindle that fits through the base of the frame rests on a nest of ball-bearings adjacent to each pedal arm. The end of the spindle is tapered so as to accommodate the shoulder of the pedal arm, and there it fits snugly, secured by a bolt which is screwed into the spindle. The bolt had fallen off and I pulled the pedal arm away from the spindle with my hand. Still there wasn't a problem because I had in my panniers a special spanner which would quickly ease a spare bolt into the spindle and fasten on the pedal arm. The spanner was not in my tool bag. I checked the innerbags, dragging out spare clothes, my passport, a couple of hats, a spare water-bottle, but I didn't find that spanner. Neither of my panniers held that stupid instrument, and the horrible irony was that it was so ridiculously important I could go no further without it. Then I remembered, it was almost certainly in Norseman, one and a half day's ride away. The only time during the journey that I had attempted to check over my equipment, I had misplaced an item which was no less important than a River Jordan document or an Indian visa. As the wind blustered the sand around my feet, I sat down in the middle of the road and held my head in my hands.

Mundrabilla wasn't far away, a lorry-driver would surely have some tool I could use to rectify the problem. So after loading up my baggage, I slipped my left foot into my left pedal and began to scoot across the Nullarbor Plain using my right foot as propulsion. As I passed the scrub-bushes and dead kankaroos at a third the usual speed, the salty smell of the sea and the rot of cankerous flesh lasted all the longer in my nostrils. Under the blue sky where lucky birds flew, I laughed aloud at the absurdity of a world record throttled-down to slow motion. In this way two hours passed, then three and not a lorry in sight. Mundrabilla was perhaps thirty miles away and the South Australian border at Eucla another fifty. Pushing and scooting with my left leg and then my right, I carried on for what seemed like hours. As my legs ached and strained, I swopped positions from one side of the bike to the other. I imagined what cyclists of the world would say whenever they found out how one per cent of the Nullarbor Plain had been traversed. Suddenly I heard the sound of a lorry brake behind me only to draw up alongside.

The driver wound down the window, 'yer not goin' to get round the world in 80 days like that,' he said and I was amazed he knew what I was doing. 'Saw you on the tele a few days ago, put it on the back and I'll give you a lift, nobody will know.'

He was wrong, he would know, I would know, and that was two people too many. On the other hand, if I carried on like this I would never make up the lost time, and it was a stupid mistake which had immobilised me, quite different to my being incapable of completing the journey. None of his tools came close to fitting my very specific bolt so I decided to accept his offer. As long as I deducted the distance covered in the lorry from the total distance cycled, this would not be considered cheating. In a journey of this nature there are so many factors to be taken into consideration, so the definition of a world record is not so strictly defined. However, there have to be reasonable guidelines and I would think that hitch-ing a lift perhaps once or twice throughout the whole journey and then only for a few miles and in an absolute dire emergency would be acceptable. In as much as the *Guinness Book of Records* ratify such journeys, it has to be left to the travellers themselves who with commensense help to make up the rules.

An hour later we pulled into the roadhouse at Mundrabilla, but the lorry park was empty. Sitting in front of a steaming mug of coffee I was imbued with an overiding sense of self-reproach. I was sadder and wiser and thoroughly pissed off. Climbing back into the lorry I would get off at Eucla, 50 miles away, whatever the outcome.

On the state border where Western Australia meets South Australia, a police checkpoint slowed down the traffic and filled the roadhouse with irritable truck-drivers. Passing from one table to another I eventually found a driver who thought he could assist me. Sure enough he had a spanner that fitted and loading up my panniers with bread, chocolate and milk, I carried on east. It was 110 miles to the Nullarbor roadhouse and it was one o'clock in the afternoon.

All that afternoon I pedalled, slowly, with the wind, hour after hour until 50 miles became 80, eventually reaching 100 since lunch. There was a little further to go before I could rest. Halfway across the Nullarbor I was getting tired and I could record the day's events in my diary no longer. It was hard to think. Even the rhythm of the journey could not combat absolute fatigue. I was starting to succumb to creeping pain. I didn't quite reach the Nullabor roadhouse where I had intended to sleep and, rolling into my sleeping bag I was too tired to eat.

Day 46 ended 150 miles later in Penong and in the afternoon of *Day 47*, I munched doughnuts and coffee, having ridden 80 miles that morning. I had crossed the Nullarbor and the day's mileage could revert to a more manageable 160 miles. Cycling less, these last two days, allowed me to recover almost completely. Although such desperate pacing seemed nonsensical, I had played a psychological game with myself and won. The journey was beginning to hurt now and I realised that there was no need to cycle over 200 miles in one day.

All morning of *Day 47* it rained. For eight hours, a storm whip-lashed the tumble-weed viciously and blew me from one side of the road to the other. After riding the usual 100 miles by mid-afternoon, I tramped into a miserable looking café on the junction of the road leading to the township of Iron Knob. Before sitting down to something to eat, I undressed in the outside toilet and wrung the clothes I was wearing as dry as I was able, and then put them back on again.

'Greetings cobber, you've just entered the land of Oz.'

As I peered over the top of the toilet door, a fellow wearing a pink tee-shirt embroidered with snow-capped mountains, also sported round black ski specs, a walkman and a multi-coloured umbrella.

'It happened in a fit it did, me dressed like this. I'm what you might call something between a disco-turd and a pooftaburger.' He turned to go, 'you don't have to stay in there. They will let you eat inside the actual café, unless of course you have something specific to do.'

'I think I've done it thank you,' I said, opening the door.

'The name's Werner, and I'm Australian' he said laughing as he stretched out his hand, 'and you're English and that's even funnier.' He clutched his sides as I was about to shake his hand. 'Did you hear about the plane-load of Poms? When the engines stopped it carried on whining.'

That was particularly unfunny I thought, and I'd heard it before. The coffee arrived, as did an enormous piece of fruit cake, which Werner claimed had been picked from one of the fruit cake trees, a speciality of Iron Knob, and he laughed. Everything I said to him made him laugh and when I suggested he looked like a fruit cake tree, he laughed even louder.

'Are you a Sagittarian?' he said, 'because all Sagittarians are adventurous, are you?'

I told him I probably must be.
'When did your moon rise?'

I had no idea.

'Well, it was probably ascending, because if it was going down, you'd be as loopy as a dingbat, and you'd be going across here on a vacuum-cleaner and a pair of roller-skates instead of a stupid old bike.' He laughed, and without knowing why, so did I.

Werner was the first person I'd sat down with and spoken to for 600 miles. On his face was a smile that had stuck long after an amusing thought had come and gone. Now Werner was suddenly quiet. It was as if I wasn't there, and as his head began to loll to one side, his eyes rolled and he was in fear of falling off his chair. There was no more conversation left in this Australian. Saying goodbye to Werner, who was now asleep, I wrapped myself up in my waterproof coat and carried on in the rain. There remained about 70 miles left to ride before I could rest for the evening. The road was long and

straight and boring. The miles ticked past at their own sweet pace, I would have delighted in spending some time in the land of Oz. Instead I had to settle for the sight of a flock of migrating birds. Round and round they swooped, forming at once the shape of a square, then a cigar and finally fanning as they found their direction and headed off to some far distant place. As evening fell, the lights of Port Augusta wavered in the distance.

After a quick meal of hamburgers and chips in a fast food restaurant, it was time to leave Port Augusta. I found it difficult readjusting to people after having had time quite alone, so didn't make any attempt to talk to anyone. Instead, not too far on the road to Adelaide, I decided to ride past the outskirts of town and find an old drainpipe in which to sleep. The sounds of young boys playing football in the Trotting Club echoed in the distance.

The road to Adelaide was due south and, as I had ridden 180 miles with the benefit of a westerly breeze, the crosswind shook me abruptly in the darkness. The rain began to lash and I again began to feel exhausted. There was not a scrap of shelter under which to crawl, so I plodded on. As the wind strengthened, the wet entrails of lorries, bespattered and mucky, sucked and sprayed me in a darkness that was now pitch-black. I looked back at Port Augusta, and was awed. I stood in the rain to stare. In the distance, a power-station looked like a Mississippi steamboat, docked into town for a party. Strung from bow to funnel from the top of the deck to the stern, the most gaily coloured lights bristled and beamed. A column of white smoke indicated the engines were running and in my mind I imagined the testy refrains of a jazz-band trumpet lacing guests together in a flap and a whirl. Having coincidently stopped by an old building sloshing about with the sounds of a water-pump, circulating sewage, I heard the shrill squeal of rats. There was nowhere to sleep and it was raining and cold. In my mind I toyed with the image of the steamboat. Below deck, pink and yellow taffeta would ride up the thighs of ladies out of breath, whilst moustachioed men in top hat and tails wound their palms distractedly around the heads of silver-topped canes. Turning to continue into the night, an oncoming trucker flashed his lights at me and I knew all he would see was the reflection of his headlights in my eyes. I was so vulnerable. After 185 miles in the wind and the rain I was no longer in complete control of my senses. Wobbling along in the darkness, I was vaguely aware of the Adelaide train rushing past with the silhouetted figures of passengers leaning forward to look out into the storm. As I glanced back, the steamboat continued to play the refrains of a swinging good time, whereas I could continue no longer.

I had decided that wherever I was I would sleep. To slip in the rain could mean my death. Climbing off my bike, I turned around and saw a light shining through a small copse of trees. It was a house, and had I not stopped, I wouldn't have noticed it. Holding onto a white gate overlooking a small garden, I saw two boys sitting in front of a small fire. An older man entered and patted one of the boys on the head and that gesture gave me the encouragement I needed to ask for the use of a garage in which to sleep.

'No you don't,' he said without a moment's hesitation, 'you'll come and have some snap and sleep on the floor by the fire.' The relief on my face must have been noticeable, but only another traveller on the road would understand what it's like to be dragged in from the cold. I was brought in front of the fire and the lady of the house handed me a cup of tea.

Having washed and changed, I ate rabbit kebabs with a bottle of 1980 vintage Aussie Port. After ice-cream and chocolate topping, I was shown the snooker room and given a tour of a thousand English beer mats that decorated the walls. I was so obviously fatigued that little was asked of me in return, least of all conversation, but I tried. Before long, everyone retired to bed and I laid out my sleeping bag by the fire. Today's ride had hurt me. As I drifted off to sleep a hundred thoughts crashed around my head. Beginning to drift off to sleep I thought of my seven days across Australia. I can ride nearly 165 miles each day with a little more effort needed in the rain. I have smelt the rotting carcasses of forty-seven kangaroos and two trampled wombats and have learnt the essentials of passing conversation punctuated with 'stubbies and no worries'. That is all I know so far about this large and pleasant land.

For most of the following day it rained. By mid-afternoon I had decided to make full use of a strong tail-wind and try and reach Adelaide. There was a fair chance that was too difficult a task to achieve and as I was still in the throes of a decision, a car pulled up alongside me and a decision was made for me. A family driving home invited me stay on their farm around the corner. Following the car over a rough track off the main road we reached a house where window shutters banged and horses clopped around the yard. The rhythm of the journey was embedded in my mind and the strain showed in my eyes.

At five o'clock the following morning I breakfasted before setting off yet again in the dark. Again, it was raining but I was warm inside and the wind blew me south to Adelaide. Today was *Day 49*, and I was three-quarters of the way across Australia.

The manager of the Adelaide Hilton was my host here and after meeting a couple of local newspapers and radio stations, I retired to my room to wash and change. In such clean warmth I could look out over rooftops getting dark. Switching on the television I was stunned watching the aftermath of an aircraft crash on the runway of my home town of Manchester. Uganda was recovering from a coup and in Beirut, another thirty-eight people had been killed. In New York, a lottery was in process whereby the lucky ticket holder would receive $58 million. Two previous beneficiaries were being used in adverts to sell the tickets. Luc Eisenhower was black and a light-bulb fitter until he won $5 million. He was no longer poor therefore it no longer mattered that he was black. Curtis Sharp was portly in his new pink silk suit, and as the television announcer quite rightly said, 'with $5 million he could now divorce his wife and marry the girl of his dreams.'

Looking at my map and counting the miles recorded in my diary, the total distance cycled to date was approximately 8,600 miles in 49 days. The back of the diary had been reserved for the signatures of people having seen me cycle through their locality. Some people searched me quizically when I asked them to sign my book, trying to find a loop hole in my sanity, others

laughed and obliged readily but no-one refused such an innocent request. I had also collected addresses and sent postcards to my Dad from most of the major cities of the countries I'd passed through. The verification of a world record, had to rely on a little common sense and my integrity. I folded my map and switched off my light and went to sleep.

The last quarter of my journey across Australia would take me across the barren flatlands of the Plains of Hay. It was around 1,000 miles to Sydney and I had six days in which to cover the distance. If the wind was behind me, then it would not be too difficult, even taking into account my present state of fatigue. If the wind blew against me from the east, the complete lack of shelter grinds a cyclist to a standstill in a matter of miles.

From Adelaide I passed north through Gawler before turning east again and onto the Murray River flood plain ending up in the small town of Bembura. The next day would hopefully place me in the township of Euston after which I would reach the centre of the Plains in Hay itself, on *Day 52*. To cross 1,000 miles of flat featureless territory, it is necessary to create landmarks of your own. Towns positioned equi-distant across this gulf would give me an attainable goal each day. It was no longer possible to understand properly my whereabouts. This was Australia and I was cycling across a huge continent on the way to somewhere else. But the journey had disintegrated. Days were no more than numbers, and countries contained the miles across which I had to cycle, and there were still 4,250 miles yet to be covered in the 30 days that remained. It was impossible to evaluate this around the world record simply as a start and a finish.

On the outskirts of the town of Bembura, I crossed the Murray as the day slowly began to turn yet again into night. Again, the day's end was coloured with the intensity of the effort of having ridden 150 miles. The waters were still, almost dead. The river flowed slowly and gracefully and tree trunks stuck out of the mirrored surface. Dead and standing upright, these trees could have been mistaken for those that stand in a swamp. Reflected between such sticks of ashen-grey, clouds were red-rimmed like eyes having shed tears. Perhaps by tomorrow everything would be alright, the clouds would be white and the sky quite blue, the tears would have been blown away. The river-edge foamed, in anger, maybe it was frustration, but looking over the bridge I could see a reflection of myself.

Hovering around a greasy café I asked an old lady if she knew where I might stay for the night.

'You can come back to our place if you like,' she said without the slightest hesitation. 'I'll give you a good meal, some wine, and I'll bring a journalist friend of mine to interview you.' So surprised at such openess I hardly spoke. 'Come on, follow me,' and she jumped into her car and drove along the main street with me tailing behind. It was dark as I cycled towards her house. A stranger in my own country would probably not have been invited home at night. I cycled hard, turned left, and sweeping around a couple of right hand bends we were out of town. The road was rough and the red brake lights of the car lit up whenever I was out of sight. Passing through a gate we came to rest along a muddy track by the lighted window of a small house. The old lady got out of the car and intro-

duced herself as Valerie. Her husband Ian appeared at the door. He and I sat and talked as Valerie laid the table for dinner. Suddenly it occured to me it was Saturday. I was just in time to phone the *Saturday Picture Show*.

'Oh, you're going to phone the other side of the world, and from my house, how exciting, can we all listen?'

As usual I would reverse the charge. Tonight I would be broadcasting live to the two and a half million viewers who were following my progress. I imagined that for every person who admired this journey as an achievement, there would be as many who thought it a waste of time. As Jack, the sound engineer, tuned me into the studio, I listened to the rumblings of the programme. What would 'Top Cat' be getting up to this week? Would Benny ever manage to outwit 'the Boss'? Would Mark, the presenter, forget who I was and what exactly I was doing? The countdown began; five, four, three, two, one and I was 'on' live to the majority of the children of the whole of the United Kingdom. Three minutes later I was 'off'.

Sitting down to my first taste of red wine since leaving Glossop, I heard Ian use the phone to call a journalist friend. Before long an old lady, dressed like Agatha Christie's Miss Marple, joined us to eat.

'I want to interview you for the Church magazine dear,' she said, rummaging around her handbag for a pen. 'Ah, here it is. Now dear, tell me how it all began...'

My heart sank. I've told my life story to so many journalists that all its feeling has been lost. Sometimes cycling around the world becomes a job, as mundane and repetitive as the most mundane of occupations. As we talked, the aroma of food being cooked distracted me. Waiting for dinner in a kitchen smelling of chicken and oranges was as unforgettable as anything I'd ever experienced in a 100,000 miles of cycling.

'That is the most incredible smell I've encountered on my journey so far.'

'What is?' The dowdy lady enquired, a little taken aback.

'The oranges and chicken, you want to write about that, far more interesting than me.'

Slightly miffed at my indifference to the journey she put her pen in her bag and turned to talk to Valerie.

The oranges were tangy, the chicken and salad served with lashings of gravy was delicious, and after fruit cake and custard, I had eaten as much as I could. They had a famous test cricketer for a grandfather, Nip somebody or other. The vines were doing well. And what about the EEC? And what about the Aussie war effort? We drank a couple of glasses of home made wine. Ian had an acre of vines tangled around the front of the house. The silver plated tea service was installed in front of a roaring log fire and later a bottle of the finest Australian claret pleasantly warmed the palate. This was cycling around the world with style. This was comfort itself on the far side of the world. Not only was I warm with drink and a satisfied belly, I was alive. Just occasionally, during a moment of real relaxation in this, the hardest of all my adventures, I could sit back and think things to be a little under control.

The following morning was *Day 51* and I said goodbye before the sun had risen. Today I had planned to ride around 170 miles before the sun set. I actually rode 168 miles in 10 hours. All morning the wind blew a gale from the north-west, and turning to gust from the west, it hurled me east with a fury.

On such a day, the impossibility of vast distance is much less frightening. The legs still ache and at first the heart beats heavily, clumsily even, until at last, the rhythm is regained. The breathing becomes more regular, less intense, and the circular action of the legs begins to massage the muscles and help squeeze away the pain. Cycling with the wind, riding at the speed of a slow motorbike eases the effort. Cycling into a hard wind is devastating. When the wind fights you every inch of the way, every action of every muscle in the body is utilised to force through the battering. One supreme gust would destroy my momentum and the bike and I would come to a standstill. Only by running alongside the bike and leaping onto the saddle could I build up enough speed to overcome the strength of the wind. It would have been impossible to continue around the world in 80 days had the wind been any less in my favour. But there were so many factors that could terminate such adventure; the distance, fatigue, injury, death, boredom, home-sickness, madness, mechanical breakdown, the heat, the rain and the wind.

The effort needed to cover vast mileages is rewarded by the exhilaration of the speed of the wind pushing me faster. Seventeen miles per hour is a good average after being on the road for nearly two months on a bike loaded with the equipment for an adventure. At such a speed the journey seemed easy. There was no pain. After 150 miles, with only one stop and a few seconds of human contact, there was nothing in my mind other than a feeling of well-being and a manic outburst of laughter. Every 20 miles or so I would erupt into an uncontrollable hysteria that lasted for a few brief seconds. Instantly I could feel my face contort in pain, the masochistic pleasure of which was indescribable.

After a short stop for lunch in a roadhouse nearly 80 miles from anywhere, I carried on, panting gently as I pedalled continuously. Adjacent to the road, thousands of acres of sleeping wheat fields in the barren landscape waited for the demise of winter. The road stretched ahead of me as it had done for thousands of miles. As I turned to look behind, the sight was the same. Rolling in front of me like a fast moving carpet, a white line was separated by a short patch of grey tarmac. The further I looked, the closer the line became, until far far away, the single dotted line that was to stretch from one end of a thousand miles to another, joined up with the sides of the road on the horizon. If only once I could catch up with the horizon, I would at least think I was getting somewhere.

Around mid-afternoon, I saw a van full of people parked on the side of the road. I asked them if they could spare a drink of water.

'We'll give you more than a drink of water if you make it to Mildura,' one of them said with a knowing look and they all burst into laughter.

'We're actresses, and I can tell you, everyone of these girls knows how to do a quick scene change,' another added suggestively.

'Off with his pants,' someone screamed from the back of the bus.

'I've just ridden 130 miles, I don't know if I can manage you all at once,' I called back cheekily.

'Did you hear that girls?' the third girl shouted, turning to her mates, 'he doesn't want to play,' and in a mock gesture of disappointment they all groaned. Peering through the driver's window I laughed, 'I've got to go on, hope you're not too upset?'

'Upset, we're devastated!' said the girl nearest the window, 'but I suppose we'll have to make do somehow,' and she winked knowingly.

The girls were a tease and I was enjoying every saucy minute. Saying goodbye seemed such a waste but I had to go on. They hadn't any water but they did give a carton of fruit juice which I drank cycling along the dusty road. Eventually catching me up, the bus slowed down and they all leaned out of their windows. 'Eh, Pommie,' one of the girls shouted, 'wherever you end up tonight have a good one and grab an eyeful of this.' As the rest of the girls whistled the striptease song, slowly and seductively she pulled off her teashirt and blowing me the sexiest of kisses, pressed herself against the window.

The day was quiet and the afternoon warm, so feeling a little tired, and because traffic on this quiet Australian highway amounted only to several cars and a handful of lorries each day, I lay down in the middle of the road. Looking up at the sky I saw high clouds ripple in the same way a beach wrinkles after the tide goes out. Yet, the sky was so blue it reminded me of the sea. As a child I spent a long weekend each year in Blackpool, where the sea is always murky-grey. Here, I could hear the throaty squawks of green parakeets as they perched on trees lining the road. The warm air was full of the sound of flapping wings as they continually adjusted their position. The scent of lavender perfumed the balmy air, so sweet it was sickly, mixed with the acrid smell of pitch warming in the sun.

Riding into the small town of Euston, I wheeled my bike up to the General Store and sat down in front of a couple of hot meat pies and a steaming cup of coffee. I seemed to be eating less now, riding 14 hours a day, than before the training for the journey started. It didn't make biological sense to me using more energy than at any other time of my life and eating nothing here to compensate. I should have lost weight rapidly. Yet still I wasn't a skeleton, my weight having deviated by less than half a stone.

Two fellows and a girl in horse-riding jodhpurs were browsing through a shelf of videos. They were loud and abrasive, I was nervous and silent. The shrieks of a girl startled me. Another fellow entered the shop, with a stubbly chin and an extended waistline that separated a dirty tee-shirt from a pair of ragged jeans. Picking up a soft-porn movie he paid his money, and the girl in jodhpurs sniggered, trying to contain another shriek. He rushed out in embarrassment and she laughed. As I sat there acclimatising myself to human contact after another day alone, and without speaking, I wondered why I'd bothered to seek out other people.

Sitting in that café so far away from home I remembered something Gurdjieff wrote about life being seen as an accidental collocation of atoms, and that the only rational attitude is one of unyielding despair. It was difficult for me to feel always positive about this adventure. Every moment of ecstasy on the journey meant I had to wade through the insipid and the stale. Exhilaration would arrive unexpectedly in the middle of a barren landscape or the crowded street of big city. Then would come the low after the high.

Leaving the café I pushed my bike across the road. I looked up at a group of stars as I laid out my sleeping bag at the base of a giant wheat silo. Feeling as I did, the size of this man-made object had more impact on me than a cluster of lights a million light years away. By that silo, the loneliness and the darkness no longer had their previous impact and I sheltered in the midst of something I understood. Lorries continued to shine into the night, their shadows climbing up the walls of the silo only to disappear. The night breeze gusted and whined before falling silent, and my face was now cold. I had succumbed. I thought of my Dad drinking his homebrew on the other side of the world. He would be thinking of me in much the same way I was thinking of him. I thought of a lady I thought I had loved. The warm curve of her smile was soft and welcoming, like the warm curve of her white satin thighs. The understanding we had for each other was almost telepathic. Would she be thinking of me now, as I was of her? Under the support of a tower so tall I felt stronger. The strain of the journey had taken its toil. A tear crept onto my cheek and I creased my eyes and waited. I willed something to happen. A moment passed, it was too late. Whatever I wanted to feel had been lost.

The following morning was warm and dry, it was *Day 52* and I hoped to reach the town of Hay. Cycling for 150 miles took me well into the afternoon. An old pick-up clattered past with a couple of farm dogs hanging on the back for all they were worth. The van screeched to a halt after which three men tumbled out. I looked behind me, ready to make a U-turn. One of the fellows clutched a bottle of beer and as I slowed down ready to bob and weave they walked quickly towards me.

'Good on yer mate, yer the forth mad bikie we've seen this year, but yer still deserve a drink, we won't hold it against yer.'

The taller of the three smiled and held the bottle.

'Go on, I know we live in the middle of bloody nowhere, but we ain't gonna eat yer.'

I took the bottle, wiped the lip and swigged. A younger fellow slapped me on the back and I was given another beer.

'This, stubbie,' the young one said pointing at the bottle.

'Oh don't you bother with all that yer great tit,' the taller one told his mate, 'he's a Pom an' it's, "Let's have another glass of best beer, please my man."' They all laughed at his mimicry.

'Well what do you say?' I said.

'Yer grab the bottle between yer legs and yer pull off the top with yer teeth. Yer stick it in yer trap an' yer down it all in one. Do yer get my drift sunshine?'

I nodded that I did.

'We're not all backward here yer know,' he continued, 'just most of us.'

I choked and burst out laughing. They smiled. I drank more beer and as the sun began to set, more and more I forgot about the schedule.

'The problem we got out here is a definite shortage of Sheilas. Now when you get back to Pom Land, you tell all them nice beauties to come and meet some nice boys like us,' he paused. 'Oh, yea, and tell 'em to bring their own beer,' and we roared with laughter.

Pointing to some indiscernible place on the horizon, they said small communities were having the time of their lives.

'We don't need the city people here, matey, we know what we're about. Have a few drinks, have a dance, have a few more beers, have another dance. And there lies the problem. Ten blokes to every woman, it's bloody inhuman,' he turned around, 'and another thing, I'm sick of dancing with him.'

'Yea, an' I'm sick of you too,' his mate said, 'yer've got big feet and yer stink too.'

'For us,' the tall one said, 'the world begins and ends approximately nowhere on that horizon and we wouldn't have it any other way.' Again we laughed. After four strong beers, everything began to appear funny.

'Here, put another stubbie in yer bag and keep goin' to wherever yer goin', that's my philosophy matey an' I'm stickin' to it. Cheerio and no worries eh?' At that they all climbed into the pick-up and drove away like crazy.

I carried on towards the early evening sky with a clearer idea of the face of reality; from behind the neck of an Australian 'stubbie'. An hour later I sat down in the town of Hay in a Greek fish and chip shop on the main street.

After a plate of fish and chips I rode round town looking for somewhere to sleep. The heavy wooden doors of a Presbyterian Church were slightly ajar, pushing them open I crept silently into the darkness. For a moment I could see nothing until, little by little, a chink of light entered from the outside. I could just make out the altar. Laying out my bag near the door, I remembered visiting the vicar of my own parish as a child. One of his eyes had a serious deformity and when he looked at me I was never sure whether it was me he was addressing or someone behind me. Adding to his odd appearance were a pair of round wired-on National Health spectacles which, being too small, pressed around his face. Apart from the little time he spent in the pulpit, he was never without a cigarette, a stalk of ash eventually falling on his cassock. These were fond memories as I drifted off to sleep, but the Vicar of Dinting was the beginning and end of my religious experience.

All the next day, *Day 53*, I rode with the wind. It was a 16 hour ride from Hay to my planned stop in Cootamundra. *Day 54* would last 14 hours to Goulburn and on *Day 55* I entered the outskirts of Sydney winding slowly to my first rest day since the Far East. Still the Australian part of the journey was not quite completed. In the Hilton Hotel there were journalists to meet and the following morning, a film was to be made for the *Picture Show*. In the afternoon there were more radio interviews, dinners, drinks, hellos, farewells and a plane to be boarded. In between, there were aching muscles to be rested and a very tired mind to be relaxed. I was crucially held together by a nervous energy that felt like an elastic band pulled taut. I had cycled nearly 3,000 miles since leaving Perth. New Zealand would be a time for regrouping my reserves. The next difficulty to overcome was in understanding there existed yet, the final 3,000 mile stage across America. So far it had been hard. I had reason to believe it would get harder.

That evening I was driven to the airport by the film crew who wanted to capture a little more of the journey as I checked in at the Air New Zealand desk. Placing the bike, and the panniers separately on the baggage scales, the combined weight was 18 kilos, exactly the same as when I set off from home. There was no room for souvenirs on this journey. I was tempted to stand on the scales myself to see if my weight had altered. I looked thinner now and my face, reflected in the camera lens, was tired and gaunt. Handing my ticket and passport over the desk, the crew filmed and I spoke a few words towards the camera. A boarding pass was given to me and I was allowed to proceed to the security control area. I didn't want to leave Australia. Its boyish charm attracted me and I was just getting used to the isolated settlements and the openness of the people.

8 · NEW ZEALAND

It was a two-hour flight to the South Island and I was to spend the night in Christchurch, a small city on the east coast. The following day I was to be interviewed by New Zealand's most popular children's television presenter Danny, on his bike, and Keith, the producer of the show, was to meet me at the airport. As the plane landed and then taxied in the darkness, I stepped onto a land as far away from home as it could ever possibly be. As I pushed my bike wearily into the arrival hall, someone introduced himself as Keith. I dismantled the wheels from the frame and pushed the bike into the back of his car. It was already 11 p.m. and I had to be in the studio before 7 a.m. By midnight I was asleep.

The following morning the film crew viewed Danny and me from every angle as we chatted about the adventure. I glimpsed the snowy sides of mountains that seemed faraway, 'Is that Mount Cook?' I asked Danny.

'Naw,' he said as we cycled towards the outskirts of Christchurch, 'Cooky's always covered in cloud. But you'll like Christchurch, it's very English. Course, how would I know, I've never been there?' Danny pointed out what was an old public school. 'It's a library now. Come to think of it, I've never been in one of them either.'

The crew filmed us in front of a church with a beautiful spire that over looked what Danny told me was the main square of the city.

'An I'll tell you something else as well,' and he nodded in the direction of the church, 'I havn't been in one of them for a while.' We laughed, I enjoyed his company tremendously and later that afternoon he invited me to stay that night at his house; his wife would cook me a special meal.

The journey to Danny's village was beautiful. For an hour he drove towards the crest of a mountain which he said was the lip of a crater lake. The sky was dark and stormy and when I looked hard out of the window I could just see the forms of clouds, frantically scurrying on the edge of bad weather. 'It's going to pee down,' and as soon as Danny spoke, large drops of rain began to hit the windscreen. A moment later, the full might of a storm lashed rods of rain from one mountainside to another. 'Soon be there pal, we live by the shore of that crater lake,' he pointed to a surface reflecting the lights of a small village, 'and you can eat and sleep and be ready for tomorrow.' I was tiring. There was little life left in me tonight.

After dinner I watched television for half an hour and excused myself. I was too tired to converse. It was an odd feeling sleeping in the crater of an extinct volcano, and it was even odder when I remembered that I was on the other side of the world.

The next day was *Day 58*, and after breakfast, Danny drove me back to Christchurch to the studio where our short film was shown on the live Saturday programme. After Danny, Frank Flash and Clive Crumble, the two other presenters, had finished the show, I was driven to the airport where I boarded my flight to Auckland on the North Island. Again, the plane landed and taxied in the darkness and I was tired and disorientated. I could have waited in Sydney for two days for a direct flight to Los Angeles, but although the world record is of paramount importance to me, I couldn't resist the invitation to explore a little of New Zealand.

At the arrival hall in the domestic terminal of Auckland airport I was met and driven to another hotel. The lobby was grand and impersonal and all I wanted to do was watch a late-night movie and sleep.

The next morning I awoke with the warmth of the sun on my face. The bells of a church tolled faintly and for that moment I was warm and cosy and felt as if I hadn't got a care in the world. Then I thought about tonight. I would have to fly through the night to Los Angeles, stopping briefly in Honolulu. I feared Los Angeles. I had heard about the violence on television. Western violence was obvious and blatant, it was something I understood. Violence in the east was more subtle, but every bit as terrible.

Today was the last of my vacation. The occasional spasms that occurred in my legs when resting were less intense, and the bloodshot corneas of my eyes were whiter. Until I was picked up and delivered to the airport this evening, this day of the journey belonged to me. After breakfast I stepped into the street in front of the hotel and walked across the road and into a graveyard.

This part of Auckland had fallen into disarray, grey tombstones with long faces turned on their sides, overgrown with green winter nightshade. Red wrought iron railings, brittle and flaking, leant at an angle, stained with years of rain. Concrete pillars lay round about having settled heavily under the eves of an overpass. It was Sunday and New Zealand was sheltering from the rain. So was I. As I wandered around the tombs I was quite alone. Spending so much time without company, as I cycled my 170 miles each day, I thought my desire for companionship would extend further than the maggoty remains of what I sensed were a forgotten crowd of corpses. But I too felt forgotten. So far away from home, the bonds of family and friends were stretching and should I allow them to snap, there would be no point in returning. The 'gone to lunch' feel about the city prevailed well into the evening and a light breeze scuttled sawdust from a pile of logs around my feet.

My flight to the USA departed at 10 p.m. so I had plenty of time to enjoy dinner. Having placed my order with the waitress, a bearded fellow sat at a table for two on my right, only to be joined shortly by another man, clean shaven and well scrubbed.

'A fellow Pom,' and the bearded man leaned across the table to shake my hand, 'the name's Bill, been out here twenty years but I still remember the flag, know what I mean?' I had a Union Jack badge sewn on my tee-shirt.

'This is my colleague John, we're guest psychologists on an international seminar on the nature of dreams, very, very interesting,' he said, sitting upright again.

'What do you think a 'Brit' looks like?' I said curiously.

'Its all to do with the way one comports oneself,' he said firmly, 'the eyes would be strict, the underlying character resolute and the gait erect.'

'If they walked like that and looked as you say they do, how come Brits abroad walk around with baggy trousers that hang nearly to their knees and order items off the menu in very loud voices?' I asked.

'No, no, no, you're thinking of Americans with their infernal complexes and their inherent feeling of superiority that asserts itself in a patronisingly humble way.'

I wasn't quite sure what to say, so I said nothing. Though it always amazed me how the most absurdly minimal amounts of information could be drawn out to form the most grandiose of statements. Not without a little irony, he ordered a bowl of chicken soup, in a rather loud voice.

During our conversation a couple had seated themselves by the table to my left and to my amusement I couldn't help overhearing their conversation.

'You're not inferring anything improper, I hope, are you Eve?' and a fellow with short black hair and small round glasses leaned forward towards his companion.

'Well Maxi dear, there's nothing improper in a situation if you both like doing it.' In my snatched glimpse I noticed that she had a fair complexion and blond shoulder-length hair.

'What on earth are you talking about?' and Max became a little intense.

'Well, George did take rather a shine to you, didn't he and you do have a pre-diliction for such things.' Eve smiled and continued eating.

Max reddened, twitched and looked left no doubt to find me staring intently into half an uneaten flapjack trying not to laugh.

'So can you do it?' one of the psychologists said.

'Do what?' I said sleepily.

'Get around the world in 80 days?'

'How did you know?'

'You were in yesterday's *Sun Herald* in Sydney,' and he showed me the picture of myself with the opera house and bridge in the background. I smiled to myself, the paper gave me an indication of how the real world viewed my journey. It was judged a good adventure.

'Well?'

'What?' I looked up.

'Are you going to make it?'

'I don't know,' and turning towards a window overlooking the bay my eyes glazed like the chink of sea on the horizon which began to lose its sparkle as the sun set.

As the couple on my right continued, the couple on my left had paid their bill and departed the restaurant. They left behind their paper and a small snippet recorded by Associated French Press caught my attention: 'Wellington: Malcolm Francis, aged 35, is standing trial in Napier, New Zealand, for beating his wife to death with a frozen sausage. He has denied murder.'

Before long a car came to take me to the airport. New Zealand was my longest stopover and by far the most pleasant of all my occasional stays. Being well rested I felt more than able to begin the final leg. I also longed to sleep again in the open air, but there was so much yet to do before that would possible. After checking in at the Air

New Zealand ticket desk, my bike was wheeled to the cargo hold as passengers flying to Los Angeles were advised to board. The plane was a wide-bodied Jumbo and as the engines whined and roared, we lurched forward, heavily laden with bodies, some tense, some excited, a few asleep. A large fellow came and sat next to me. 'Hello,' he said, 'I saw you wheeling yer bike and that yer was from England. I like bikes.'

'Are you a cyclist?' I asked him.

'Naw,' he said shaking his head smiling, 'I grow flowers.'

'Oh, what sort?'

'Big ones.' He paused. 'They're beautiful fings flowers.'

'What do you do with them?'

'I'm going to buy an 'Eskif.'

I looked puzzled.

'It's a motorbike, you know, Lord 'Eskif. An I'm going to motorbike up to Edinburgh.' His cheeks flapped a bit with excitement. 'I need to lose a little weight though,' and he patted his stomach. 'Thought I'd lost a kilo the other week, until I realised I'd taken my coat off.' I turned away for a moment, to look out of the window. Jumbos are like flying hotels perched as they are a little closer to the stars. The full moon shone on clouds we floated above and images, formed as shadows of reflected light, cast themselves in space. A blue-grey radience fell on the earth below. Five thousand feet below, craggy rocks meet the sea as New Zealand was left behind.

9 · ACROSS AMERICA

Refuelling took place in Honolulu, where I would have to pass through customs and immigration. For certain racial and ethnic types, the USA like Britain is one of the most difficult countries in the world to gain official entry. Being white, Caucasian and obviously fit and healthy, I wasn't even searched. A cursory glance at the passport and a few moments of pleasantries put me firmly on American soil.

The break in the journey was short and we boarded the plane once again to fly across the rest of the Pacific. A few hours later the sharp peaks and crests of the Southern Californian coastline came into view. Golden red and pitched against a clear blue sky they looked magnificent and stark. Sea-green waves lapped and sizzled on hot sandy beaches that spilled from the desert. As the plane tipped I had a clearer view of the Rockies, three cycling days away. Below the southern part of the Sierra Nevada appeared close enough to touch, its oven hot table top mountains simmering in the heat. As the plane flew along the coast of California, an almost biblical wilderness was slowly replaced by square plots of land wrapped around plaintive looking houses.

A film crew had been arranged by the BBC to record my first full day in America. A man with a moustache, fit and tanned, met me at the airport introducing himself as Bob. Bungling my bike into his customized mobile film unit, I sat back exhausted. Downtown Los Angeles was a cluster of skyscrapers dominating the flatlands and as Bob assured me, they were 20 miles away. According to my schedule I hoped tomorrow night to be in Palm Springs and I was to meet Bob and his assistant at intervals on the way.

In the meantime Bob, who had booked me a room on Sunset Boulevard, joined me for a quick drink in the foyer. Antique studio pieces represented an age of cinema graced by the likes of Katharine Hepburn and Cary Grant. Canvass backed chairs with the words 'Director' added to the cliché placed as they were next to bowls of creeping ivy and rubber plants six foot high. 'You'll have to be on the road at 5 a.m.,' Bob said, 'I just hope you get enough sleep, you look shattered.' It was night and peering through the foyer window I became aware I am either on the inside or outside of a window. Here people dashed from sidewalk to sidewalk, cars screeched as traffic lights changed from stop to go and the bodies which gave life to the 'city of angels' were all trying to get home for their television dinners.

My legs ached due to the enforced

two day rest in the Pacific and my eyes were beginning to droop sleepily. The hotels and restaurants, people and places had merged into a series of celluloid dream sequences and my mind was becoming incapable of distinguishing any more between reality and illusion.

Taking the lift to my room I leant my bike next to an enormous television and tuned in immediately to channel nine. Roger Moore was playing James Bond in *On His Majesty's Secret Service* crammed between Christie Brinkly advertising products for beautiful people to use in their beautiful lifestyles. Gold anodized table lamps impassively exuded a dull sort of glow sufficient to highlight a framed print of sycamore leaves drifting in the wind. As I looked out over the city with its bright coloured lights pinpricking the blackness, it was hard to imagine the wind blowing real sycamore leaves in Los Angeles.

The following morning I breakfasted at 5 a.m. and was on the road 30 minutes later. Bob knew my route out of LA and we planned to meet somewhere on the freeway around noon. In the meantime, I tediously passed a city with one of the largest urban sprawls in the world. It was hot and it was going to get hotter.

I pedalled through street after street for what seemed an eternity. All the time I was becoming increasingly conscious of limited time. A lazy day in Australia could just about be regained, a lost day here would probably destroy the journey. Soon my throat began to dry and sting and the noise of my pounding heart throbbed in my head. One of my greatest fears was the overloading of my body. I knew well enough that with correct amounts of sleep and good food, physical recovery ought to be assured every single day.

But my recent sleep pattern had been punctuated by flights across the Pacific and my constantly changing diet.

In the distance car exhaust fumes were visible as a yellow haze and, combined with a blue sky, tinges of turquoise edged the occasional cloud. The only way out of this city was through mucky air and lung-rotting miles of gasolene-belching freeway. Here the bicycle is not considered a means of transport, more a plaything of the poor and slightly mad.

My chain began to squeak and I didn't have the energy to oil it. Uphill the squeak was partnered by the rachet sound of a chain wearing badly on the cogs. Downhill the metered rhythm of a rusty moving part joined together with brakes that were warm with the smell of rubber. Imperceptibly the honking of cars the size of houses and the stench of dog-upturned dustbins had been replaced by ball bearings creaking in their case. The suburbs slowly turned into a freeway and that into a wide trail curving and burrowing into a shimmering desert. The brief companionship of people shuffling in streets had been replaced by the impersonal freeway all too soon.

Having planned the journey around an easier winter crossing of the Australian Nullarbor, I was about to be confronted with the tail end of a breathless American summer. It had been hot in Syria and cool ever since. I always thought of Equatorial regions as being torrid and fiery. Never having crossed the Equator on a sunny day, I was now 34° North and perspiring a pint of fluid every hour. The sky was sharp with white light, hurting my bloodshot eyes.

It was fifteen minutes past midday and as the sweat poured down my face I longed for Bob to catch me up and give me the excuse I needed to rest. I

expected every medium sized van to indicate they were pulling in to the right, drawing up in front of me to temporarily ease my aching legs. Thirty minutes later I was still pedalling, alone, arms badly reddened by the Californian sun. By 1 p.m. the freeway was silent. As I poured water, too hot to drink, over the back of my scorched neck, I could only think that it was too hot to drive. By 2 p.m., Bob eventually overtook me.

Renée, his personal assistant for today bore more than a passing

resemblence to Barbara Striesiand. After guzzling down a litre of Coke I rode, they followed, they filmed, I talked and as we entered a bar in Palm Springs the most beautiful of dusks began to fall.

'Do I look Californian?' Renée said to me as we sat around wicker basket tables drinking goblets of Mexican 'honey water', ''cos if I do then I'm glad 'cos sure as hell that's what I am,' and she laughed.

'The maguey cactus produces white 'honey water' which is a delicacy amongst the Aztecs,' Bob explained.

'Yeah, but tell him what happened to drunk Aztecs, tell him about the rabbits,' Renée winked at me and laughed again.

'In Aztec writing, the hieroglyph of a rabbit was used to denote a measure of drunkeness,' and as Bob looked at me Renée sniggered,

'Hey, lah de dah, Mister Robert Ernest, tell him how many rabbits you need to be a hero.'

'Well,' continued Bob, 'the Aztecs believed the cactus would turn into a goddess and it was a sign of disrespect to get drunk in front of her. A 20-rabbit symbol indicated you'd drunk enough to be clumsy, a couple of hundred indicated you wouldn't be able to stand up, so anyone depicted as a four-hundred-rabbit man was dead drunk and sentenced to death.'

More relaxed and a little rested I began to enjoy the company of these people. The evening was becoming magical as I realised how lonely I'd been these past two months. The ride had become so intense I could stare a charming character in the eye and just cycle on by. In my present role as a traveller on the other side of the world, I absorbed every opportunity to be with stimulating people, wishing the evening never to end.

Bob ordered more 'honey water' and Renée laughed even louder.

'You know, I can't stop smiling,' she said, 'an do ya know why, 'cos I jus' got

116

laid,' she blushed and murmured something like 'what the hell' as the freckles on her burnt nose went from russet to foxy. 'Did I ever tell you what I think about Italians, well they got big mouths and little willies and don't ask me how I know why. Here, let's drink to the British,' and she raised her glass, 'they're better than the goddam Italians, they got smaller mouths.'

'She's full of the gutter tonight,' Bob said and smiled,

'Yersee, he's smiling as well and do ya know why, 'cos he got laid too,' and she laughed.

As we talked and drank in our chairs the simple pleasure of sharing a sunset in a warm breeze in Palm Springs was breathtaking. The getting there was hard and complicated, but such an evening was one of those special moments that occur rarely in a hard adventure. We smiled because we were happy and also because we were a little drunk.

Bob looked at his watch and I knew the end of the evening was near. Renée insisted they tuck me up in bed in the desert so we drove to the outskirts of town. It was dark as I laid out my sleeping bag under the watchful eye of a full moon. The crisp arid grass shifted gently, bending and ducking as a wind rose to sweep the floor under twinkling stars. I shook hands with Bob and he rather sensitively went back into the van as I kissed Renée goodbye on the cheek. Turning to follow Bob she turned again and threw her arms around me, holding on as if never to let go. For a moment I didn't think she would and for that moment I was glad she didn't. Laughing she unclenched me, got in the van and waved as they headed off back to LA In their rear window I saw two forms silhouetted by oncoming headlamps. For a fleeting moment I wished I could have swopped places with Bob, that he would stand as I did, alone and in the dark, and I could be protected by the comfort of a loving friend.

Feeling a little heavy headed I woke at daybreak, climbed out of my sleeping bag and stood naked against the wind. There is probably a law in the American constitution that forbids round the world cyclists to walk in deserts without any clothes on.

Pedalling gently forever east, another day had been put into motion. Whilst cycling around the world, there were ingredients within each day that were the same. I get up with the sun, dress, ride, eat, drink, ride, wrinkle, tire, strain, ride, eat, drink, sink, fail, sleep.

For the next couple of days I was to be on Interstate 10, hedged in by 400 miles of motorway barriers designed to keep mad dogs and cyclists out. The rhythm needed to cycle the day's average of a 165 miles had not been established, without which it would be impossible to manage more than a few hours and not feel dreadfully sick. The road streched before me endlessly and the time available appeared so short. Always I felt on the verge of sickness or hysteria. The sun rose, the morning warmed and it was a Tuesday. The idea of today being a Tuesday meant nothing at all. Jet-lagged and disorientated, I had begun to lose the meaning of days and time. Yet life on the bike was governed by saved time, and the record-breaking nature of the journey depended on a meticulous awareness of lapsed moments.

I saw a café in the distance and as I pedalled closer I began to understand that often misquoted cliché of being in the middle of nowhere. I imagined 'nowhere' to be a place without people.

Much of the Mojave Desert is uninhabited, and signposts indicating directions for 'The Desert Center Café,' suggested there were people, here, in the middle of nowhere. Riding through a car park scattered with an assortment of cars, I leant my bike by the front door.

'In the Lord's name what are yer doin' child bi-cycling in this heat?' An old lady with a face wrinkled as a prune confronted me immediately I stepped inside. 'Yer surely must be mad fursure because fursure it's a hot day and yer've no right to tempt the Lord in this way.' She gulped down the remnants of a spirit from a small whisky glass.

I ordered a coffee and and quickly ate a hamburger, I'd be more able to talk then. 'The Lord has certainly got better things to occupy his time than watch over my antics in the Mojave,' I said jokingly.

'Bla-sphe-mee' she said very deliberately before wiping her moist lips with the sleeve of her tattered tweed coat. 'And why arn't yer wearing a hat,' she paused. 'Looksee, if yer think the Lord takes time out on Tuesdays yer'd better wear this until he gets back.' She threw me a baseball cap and I slipped it onto my very hot head.

I hardly noticed the interior of the café as I sat limply on a stool by the front counter. My whole body throbbed, pulsating inwardly with the heat I ordered another Coke.

'What did yer say yer was doin?' The old lady proceeded to do exactly what I hoped she wouldn't and sat next to me. I told her.

'I know why yer doin' it,' she said without a glimmer of the self consciousness that usually follows in a café full of listeners. 'I may proclaim the Lord but you proclaim yerself don't yer?' She didn't expect an answer.

I didn't have one.

'Yer won't find my sense of virtue lasting long in Sunday church and ninety minutes of boredom, I proclaim the Lord on Wednesdays as well.

'What,' and I nearly jumped off my chair to find her still talking. 'Yer were on another planet dear,' and funnelling her hands around her mouth as if I were deaf, shouted, 'I said I don't go to church on Sundays.'

'It's Tuesday today,' I reminded her.

'I know that, yer jerk, if he was around today I'd proclaim him but he ain't 'cos he would have given you a hat or some brains maybe 'cos yer sure are stupid,' and she smiled.

'Well, he did,' I said, 'you've looked after me, you've given me a hat,' and at that she turned away and polished off another bourbon. I'd upset her.

Back on the road, back in the sun, the luminosity hurt my eyes. The hat had a typically long American peak which I drew down over my face. All was brown baked earth and hot cacti in this dog-day summer's heat. I was feeling better and I knew that there was a job to be done.

Having ridden across the Mojave Desert four years ago, I vaguely remembered a really good restaurant not so far away. It was certainly no further than 100 miles. As the wind howled around the hills I was very tempted to shelter from the storm which was brewing. Even the occasional lorry that passed gave me a wider berth.

As usual, fatigue was building up and the time of day was approaching when I would begin to feel ill. Exhaustion was such a matter of fact part of my day, I almost knew the exact time when it would occur. After 50 miles, my legs ached, my heartbeat became regular. Between 50 and a 100 miles, I began to feel the rhythm that mechanically eased away the pain. To stop now would require a tremendous act of will to continue. At this point, I would happily spend the rest of the day drinking coffee. After cycling 100 miles and before covering 150 miles, the journey glides like a dream, effortlessly and with a spirit so carefree, the thought of the journey ending makes me sad. Thereafter, the rhythm falters, my body, usually steady, rocks from side to side. My neck, straining as if trying to pull the rest of the body forward, holds my head woodenly as if afraid to let go. All thoughts of the journey are lost, all grace of movement deteriorates. I curse the journey and I curse myself. Depending on the conditions of the day, the heat, the wind, the previous night's sleep, I climb off my bike with some control or I collapse. That determines whether I eat, or sleep where I fall.

Somewhere in the middle of a desert I should have liked to have talked to someone. I needed a dime. I hadn't any change and in the most sophisticated country in the world there wasn't a telephone for 50 miles. My head began to throb and my stomach churned. My legs became wobbly as I gripped the bike tightly. My eyelids were like metal shutters trying to close. My body wanted to seal tight against the world. I vomited over the handlebars. So many times I have had to scrape my handlebars clean.

Two hours further along the road at milepost 94, Tonapah Joe's and Alice's Truckstop presented itself over the horizon. The wind swept around a large cement building as I freewheeled to a stop. Neither smart nor well maintained, this paint-peeling concrete bunker was everything I could have asked for. Seeing a reflection in the din-

ing room window I saw someone I didn't recognise, he looked gaunt and thin and was standing next to a bike.

Turning towards the door it blew open with a clatter and was followed straightaway by a short stout man, bald as an egg, wearing round old fashioned spectacles held together with a sticking plaster.

'Curse this god-forsaken hole in the ground, why the Lord created this Goddam ass-end of the world I'll never know, and don't jus' stand there, come on in if you're comin'.'

Following him through the door which he held open for me, I'd already made up my mind he was Tonapah Joe, although I wasn't entirely sure whether it was a name or a place. After finding somewhere to sit by a window, I ordered flapjacks, maple syrup and eggs. Blinking I looked out of the window, and then I blinked again. Until some of my senses returned that's all I felt able to do.

The eating room was large enough to park trucks inside, instead, small square brown tables dotted the central area. Stretching along maple syrup stained walls, low sprung bench seats were positioned as if on a train. An occasional muffled twang would break the silence as yet another ageing spring suddenly got too old.

'Here yer are boy yer gotta eat yer grits.' Mr Joe brought me my breakfast. 'We get a lot of travellers passing through here we do, only last month a young fella came here on a bike,' he thought for a moment, 'or was it a motorbike last year? What the heck, time means nothin' in these parts I can tell you.' Apart from Joe, me and the coffee machine the room was still. Outside bundles of tumble weed raced around as the occasional pebble cracked against a pane of glass. Tucking into my flapjacks I felt relaxed and more able to untie a few thoughts.

My nose was red and sore, and because the sun always worked her way around to the south, my right arm blistered and swollen. My legs ached more off the bike than on and it sometimes took me several minutes to straighten my cramped legs after having sat down to rest.

'Makes yer think don't it,' he said, 'how we end up where we end up.' I nodded. 'Maybe it's better that we don't stop moving,' I suggested.

'Naw, that's not the way, I've tried it for most of my life, Vietnam, Korea, bin' everywhere done everythin' and I'm no better off.'

'Not very encouraging,' I agreed,

'Yer wanna enjoy it, don't think too much, the more yer think the more yer drink, and the more yer drink the more yer think yer think when yer don't think nothin' at all.' Carrying a bag of sugar he refilled a basin on the table. 'It'll kill yer, be it the drinkin' or the thinkin', nearly did me.' He walked off again leaving me to stare at my coffee.

It had been two hours since I stepped into Mr Joe's restaurant and it felt like five minutes. The storm had completely stopped and so had my legs. Wiggling the left ankle and then the right, I slowly worked up to the knees. A quick rub around the upper thighs and I managed to ease myself upright. I had 120 miles yet to ride.

It was uphill to Phoenix. Sprawling flatly and endlessly, the suburbs of the capital city of Arizona were not unpleasant. The desert, such that it was, had been replaced by industrial units, brand new and painted in the brightest of colours. Downtown, a sky-scraper covered in mirror windows dominated the skyline. Again I stopped for food on the east side of the city and I stopped for ten minutes to fill up my water bottle.

The awareness of passing time started to gnaw at me, so much so that for the first time in the journey I decided to ride at night and bought a set of lights.

Leaving Interstate 10 I continued on Highway 60 passing through Mesa, hoped to reach Globe and ended up in Apache Junction. Night was falling as I drank a carton of milk in a twenty-four hour store, trying to decide what to do. I would have gone on and really needed to, but was advised against it on account of the next couple of hours of road being badly lit, narrow, and busy with overnight trucks. The Sundancer eating house on the edge of town was, I had been told, the place where you could eat as much chicken and chips as you wanted for $3.75, and that was where I ended up.

Having washed and put on a new tee shirt I felt quite alert. Seated at a table next to mine an elderly couple sat in silence. When they heard me order my meal they asked me if I was from overseas.

'Oh, we have not been overseas,' the old lady said carefully, 'we have everything over here, besides that there's so much fighting.'

'In Europe?' I said, surprised.

'Oh yes, you have the riots and everything, I wouldn't like that at all.' She took a deep breath and went on, 'have you seen the Queen, she lives in London doesn't she?'

'I called round the other week but she wasn't in.'

'Oh, I thought you had to make an appointment.'

'No, no, she drives round London all the time in her black Rolls Royce and blank number plates; she's just like the rest of us really.'

120

The eating house was part of a larger establishment which also ran a bar, and during the course of the next ten chicken legs I witnessed three drunks fall out of the adjoining doorway only to crawl on their hands and knees and drive off in their car. I was glad I wasn't going any further tonight, and at that, paid my bill and slept under the stars in a field a little further on.

After four hours sleep I got back on my bike. There was never enough sleep and the less I was getting the more distorted my impressions of the journey became. I was also finding it harder to recover from the previous day's ride. Yesterday's and today's sometimes get mixed up and then I begin to get confused. It was dark and a sprinkling of rain fell to layer the black road with a watery reflection of the moon. As the

tyres squished and wooshed I felt quite unmoved by what lay ahead. Today was *Day 63* and there were 14 days to ride before the journey ended.

Behind, the orange lights of Phoenix crossed the horizon from end to end. On the left a tiny cluster of white lamps huddled cosily together under a black outline of the ominously named Superstition Mountains. I pedalled briskly to keep warm up a slight incline, indicating the climb up to the Rocky Mountains had begun. Phoenix was 1,092 feet above sea level and Globe reached 3,541 feet, less than a day's ride away. Within the next day and a half I would cross the continental divide, another 4,000 feet higher.

Chewing hungrily on a Danish pastry in Superior, I sat down with a group of workers who were enjoying a little early

121

morning sun. I enjoyed chatting to them, they seemed to understand the effort involved in the cycling.

'I know exactly what yer goin' through boy,' and an older fellow sat down next to me. 'We ain't got no romantic notions about working down the mine no more. Fact is, we never had. Papa worked there so we followed.'

Another fellow sat to the other side of me, he was tall and well muscled. 'Eight hours a day down that ass-hole,' he said pointing to a mountain in the distance. 'You'd think there was more to life than this.' He showed me his dirty hands, they were more than rough, they were scarred.

Across the road behind the shops and pressed hard against the Rocky Mountains there was a factory. It was red brick and derelict, complemented by a chimney which from where I sat looked familiar. There was nothing special about this factory but gazing at its grimy smokey facade I felt homesick for the chimneys of North Derbyshire. I ordered more doughnuts and drank more coffee allowing myself an extra half an hour's rest.

'Sitting on that machine for 14 hours every day would make my ass like a kicked round beef steak.' The tall man got up and beat his backside as if it were on fire. We laughed.

'Sure is a bit like working in a mine,' said the other fellow. He paused. 'Even so, just give me a cycle and just put me on them wide open plains. The factories are gonna shut down. Just give me a little more sunshine man, I wanna breathe that air.'

A young fellow spoke for the first time, quietly. 'It really must be great going around the world, yer must see so many things.'

'Why don't you go?' I asked.

The tall man sniggered, ''cos he's jus' an got himself a sweetheart and he's only jus' known how to jack off. What do yer think he'd go an do aroun' the world?' The older fellows laughed, it was funny, but this time I only smiled.

'You want to try it, you might like it,' I urged him.

'That's what I said to him.'

'Very funny,' I sneered, turning to the tall man. I was angry. Perhaps it was my being fatigued, but I knew what it was like being the butt of other people's humour. 'Maybe that's why you work in a mine because you don't want anyone to do better than you.' I immediately regretted what I said.

'Boy,' he said, grabbing me by the collar, 'you sure as hell don't understand. We got houses an' we got families an' we got children an' if we all go doin' Goddam crazy tricks like you, we got nothin'. So why don't you get on yer little bicycle and get the hell outta here?'

I was seething with anger, the humiliation was intense. I couldn't risk anything that would stop the project now. I climbed on my bike and left.

I had 2,542 miles yet to ride, and I slowly wound my way up the long climb out of Superior.

I ached and grunted as I climbed to the top of the rise but flashed past downhill on the other side, ecstatically and with abandon. Down and down, as if never to stop, I hugged the handlebars relaxed and easy. With so little time to absorb the colours and the smells I took them all in at once. Going downhill was like an acceleration of a day. Vivid greens and browns rushed into view, streaked as they were with powder-grey smoke from wood-burning fires. Plummeting at what felt like 100 miles per hour I suddenly became aware of something behind me. Glancing quickly I saw two huge log lorries fuming and screaming less than ten feet away, the gushing wind having hidden their approach. They were so close that their wheels pounded round at shoulder height. I became feverish as the hypnotic attraction of the pounding wheels rendered insensible any power of judgement I could make. As if I didn't exist, the side of the truck pinned me against the roadside barriers. I judged my speed to be over 40 miles per hour and there was less than three feet between the wheels of the lorry and the highway barriers and I had to balance in between the two. Had it not been for a lifetime's cycling with lorries like this, I would have closed my eyes and hoped they would go away, and that would have been fatal. As the first one passed, the second one followed, front end to tail and I knew he wouldn't be able to see me. On the side of the road sharp

flints lay unswept and the thought of a puncture appalled me. At that instant I hit a stone. I knew only too well how the bike might react. The back tyre exploded with such force I was hurled towards the side of the lorry. My left shoulder smashed against the back right-hand mudguard and I winced in pain as I rebounded against the barrier. My every instinct of survival was immediately galvanised into action. As soon as the fragile wheelrim became exposed to the road the tyre would shred into ribbons. Control at this speed would be impossible, I would be thrown under the lorry's deathly wheels. In the space of a second the wheel-rim chinked on the hard tarmac and again I leaned towards the side of the truck. The rear wheel had lost the tyre completely. I was terrified but I had to remain calm and relaxed, I tried not to think of the lorry. Normally I can freewheel down a long hill at 50 miles

per hour and not deviate two or three feet from the barrier. The awareness of the danger was too absolute and by not thinking about the lorry being so close I had a chance. My back wheel was snaking from side to side and I was nearly out of control. A gap in the barrier appeared a short distance away and braking gently I made ready to turn. The lorry was roaring as I made the minutest of movements to stay upright. A tense body now would throw me under the wheels. Switching violently I threw myself into the gap, closing my eyes, throwing my arms around my face to protect my head. With a thud and the faint smell of blood I landed heavily on soft padded grassland. I was stunned. Blood oozed from my nose as I managed to drag myself towards a tree on which, with difficulty, I could lean. In the distance, the backend of the lorry sparked and scraped round a sweeping wide bend. I took a few deep breaths, and as the warm sunshine filtered onto my face through flickering leaves, I wondered what might have been. Apart from the tyre the bike was undamaged and shaking myself into action, I eased myself onto my saddle and cycled on to the bottom of the hill.

Before long I was within shouting distance of Salt River Canyon, the memory of which, unlike the Mojave, was not lost in the land of forgetfulness. Four years ago I climbed the valley in the ghostly dead of a moonless night. A harmonica sounded the blues. Laughing and singing at the Top of the Mountain café two boys and a girl were waiting to see the dawn. We drank and ate and talked and touched, but then like now I always had to get back on the road. As I approached this beautiful valley on a sunny afternoon the café was a ruin and my briefly found friends were as ghosts.

Cottonwool clouds scurried round the warmth of the sun. Layers of granite and limestone stratified steep sided walls which looked as if they reached the centre of the earth. Clumps of red cyclamen were shaded under the barriers on the side of the road. Common blue butterflies fluttered and landed to nibble the edges of end of summer dried leaves, slightly pre-empting autumn. Next to the leaves, half a town of ants hurtled across hot tarmac, heave-hoing an apple core on their shiny black backs. Overhead a slate-grey sparrowhawk hung on the wind crying out 'kek-kek-kek' for a warm blooded dormouse. Hot and closed in, the river looked icy cool but time had become so precious I dared not even dip my toes. My paranoid fear of losing grip on myself and the journey was complete. Time would simply not slow down, least of all for a world record. In a small store at the base of the canyon, I allowed myself 15 minutes to pretend to be an Englishman having afternoon tea. I put my head in my hands because I was exhausted.

Having already ridden 120 miles since 4 a.m. that morning, I persevered for another 60. After 16 hours on the road, I began to feel very tired indeed. The race had been on for a while but each short passing day occasionally lasted an eternity. Each day I gave all my strength, my spirit and every second of my existence to ride around the world in 80 days. I was not going to let it slip out of my grasp easily. Freewheeling into the neat wide streets of Show Low at 8 p.m. in the evening, I found a fast food restaurant and bought a hamburger and a drink of Coke. Just behind the police station I located a rather nice chestnut tree still brown and red. Leaning my bike under the boughs I laid my sleeping bag

124

alongside and, giving the stars a weary passing glance, slept.

As early morning mists were beginning to clear I wiped clean sleepy eyes. Nights ran into days and days into nights as *Day 64* presented itself, marginally separated from *Day 63*. Three hours down the road in a coffee shop in Springerville I thought I might be happy. It was breakfast time and a major highlight of my day due to the distinct possibility someone might actually talk to me.

The first thing I noticed was a poster hanging askew above the coffee machine. A photograph depicted a pig balancing on a wall underneath which was a quotation from Virgil, 'they that think they can, can'. The second thing I noticed was a waitress with beautiful brown hair cascading over her shoulders, eyes as black as a new moon and

lips that were full and luscious. Not a moment too soon, she took my order and quickly returned with hot cakes and syrup, ham and eggs sunnyside up. I felt like the pig, it was feeding time again.

Getting up to leave, the waitress came to pour me my ninth cup of coffee. As we chatted it was obvious she wasn't thinking about pouring the coffee and neither was I. The cup overflowed into the saucer. She apologised and flushed, and when I said it was all my fault she looked away and in a fluster filled three discarded empty cups on the table next to mine.

Climbing higher in the sunshine it all felt so easy. Not an ache not a moan and the bike was as smooth as the wind. The Continental Divide was not very far away and being the highest point of the Rockies between the Yukon and here,

it divided the western seaboard of the USA from that of the east. A warm feeling gushed inside me for no particular reason, I was 90 miles down on the most optimistic schedule and had yet to cross another nine states in all. Mile after mile passed by and I was hardly breathing. Late morning came and went without a moment's break as did early afternoon. The signpost of Pie Town came into view and I touched the ground for the first time since breakfast and walked into possibly the most famous teashop on the length of the Continental Divide, the Brake 21 café.

As I savoured the delights of a slice of coconut cream, a couple of tramps sat down next to me. I had not spoken a single word for ten hours, and they were a definite infringement of my privacy. The lady with the dirty fingernails turned away from her companion, 'You're English aren't you?'

Sighing, I grunted, in the most unenthusiastic of murmerings, something like I suppose so.

'I knew it, as soon as you walked in I simply knew it,' and she clasped her hands together with rapture.

I felt a little guilty and asked her more politely how she knew.

'The English have the finest of features, it's a characteristic you know, it stems from the long lines of incestuous ancestry.'

My fork clattered on the plate. 'Oh, yes, you only have to look at the fine lines of the Huguenots, look at their noses, they are all the same, long and straight.

I knew we would chat for less than an hour but I had a feeling the conversation was going to be enchanting. She had limp grey hair, dirty and dishevelled, her eyes were amongst the saddest I'd ever seen. She said she was the

Queen of England's sister on account of their sharing the same birthdate.

'The only difference between us that I can detect,' she said ' is that I want to write a really porno book with everything in it, and her Royal Majesty probably won't have the time to read it.'

Her companion had the most transparent blue eyes and he seemed incapable of fixing his gaze for longer than a blink.

'Do you ever think of nothing?' he said,

'It's a funny thing you should say that,' I replied, 'in actual fact I do, why do you ask?'

'Oh nothing,' he replied and I saw a little glint in his eye.

'Don't be abstract darling,' she said before turning to me, 'Charles is so stuffy and Di's such a snob. My husband is Philip, Jack Philip,' and she laughed. 'Pass me a cigarette darling,' and she imitated how she thought the Queen would sound with her overlong vowels.

'Yer darn bastard, I luv yer,' and Jack pursed his lips.

'Oh 900 kisses darling,' and as the drama unfolded especially for me, she held out her hand.

'I love my wife so much it hurts, when I smack her round the head, it really hurts.' Married for six months after a whirlwind romance they were obviously terribly in love. His arms were covered in sores having been rooting around rubbish dumps for something to sell.

'King of the Dumps we are,' said Jack, 'not a broken down pram left unturned. A little girl started talking by the window and he turned to look.

'And just make sure you're looking and that's all,'

'I like looking at little girls,' he said defensively.

'I know, and so do lots of men. It's just that you're more honest than them. He does go to burlesque shows though,' and she sniggered to me, 'because he needs all the help he can get.' That had made Jack Philip angry and to appease him she decided they should go for a walk. Bidding me goodbye they paid their bill from a wad of ten dollar notes that looked like a lifetime of savings. Outside, they fondly remonstrated with each other and as they walked away she turned round and looked at me through the window. Placing her finger to her nose she winked.

In order to reach Magdalena that night I rode all afternoon without stopping. After four hours of pedalling through soft rolling hills, a wall of mountains eventually jutted into view, rising around the edge of a plateau like the wall of a crater lake. Reckoning the base of the mountains to be about 15 miles away, I decided not to try to cross them tonight. The road was as straight as a vapour trail. On either side of the road, tufty fields stretched to the base of mountains that seemed to sit on the horizon. Dropping behind me in all her gilt-edged splendour, the sun sent ginger streaks of sunshine to enliven oppressive outcrops of rock. I thought of my Dad. On his seventieth birthday he made two things known; that he intended drinking his home-brew until he was nailed in his coffin and that he understood 90 per cent of everything, 'but it's the last ten per cent I want to know,' he said, 'that's the meaning of life, that's what I'm working on.'

On my right the national observatory of America's radio telescopes formed into two intersecting axial lines. I imagined someone watching me so I pedalled a little faster.

The rhythm of the day was fading but

still, the long wide road concentrated my efforts and strenghtened my thoughts. I thought of John Lennon when he said, 'well here I am rich and famous just like I always wanted to be, and nothing's happening'. Whilst fame might be necessary to proceed in a world inhabited by people exhibited as celebrities, I still thought it an over-rated indulgence. Dad was always paraphrasing parts of the Bible, 'whatever is given is also taken away'. Fame, it seems to me, certainly comes into that category. Someone once said of fame that it was, but a twinkle, that popularity was mere chance and the only thing of any certainty was oblivion. Being only 13 days from the end of the journey I wondered if my life would change when I returned home. I felt much the same now as I did when the journey began.

Today had been long and tiring. It hurt. The road stretched ahead of me and I seethed with contempt. Contempt for myself for considering such a desperate journey, the journey itself for being so hard, and today for being so boring. For once in my journey I wished this long wide road that carried me to nowhere would go to Hell.

As old blisters on my feet and hands opened up and suppurated, salt from my forehead stung the whites of my eyes. Sometimes I was relieved beyond reason to have blisters. Whenever I tried to think my way out of a vacuous existence, it made my head ache. Blisters took my mind off matters that it was easier not to be concerned about. I ought to be in the pub drinking pints of beer watching all the girls sitting with their arms crossed watching all the boys. I'd ask for a quick dance and one of the girls would turn to her mate and giggle, her boyfriend would sidle alongside bristling. That reminded me of a *Peanuts* cartoon in which Snoopy was sitting under a cactus beside a long straight road. It read,'I should go into Needles tonight...I can see the bright lights beckoning me...Maybe I'd see a cute chick, and I'd say to her, 'Hey, how'd you like to go play video games?'

At that moment, a boyfriend appears in the cartoon and threatens to pound Snoopy into the ground.

Looking disconsolate, all Snoopy could say was, 'Sitting in the desert on a Saturday night talking to a cactus isn't so bad....'

On this long boring road with pin-pricks of light that never seemed to get any closer, I felt angry. I expected more from the journey than it could give me. Cycling around the world had left me in a state of exhaustion with no more than a pocketful of thoughts, half formulated and wild. I felt as if the road had dealt me a crushing blow. At 5.35 p.m., less than two weeks before the end of the journey, I was resigned to think that this adventure had given me less than I had hoped. Any meaning of life that I didn't understand before the start, was as shrouded in mystery now as it was then. And yet, however hard and unreasonable the demands of an adventure, if I were forced to abandon it, I would rather cycle to the edge of the road and drop off the end of the world.

Getting dark all of a sudden, the flickering white phosphorescent lamps of Magdalena came to life, leading me to the main street. This afternoon seemed to have lasted all day and this last hour all afternoon. The darkness brought the cold and I put on two woolly jerseys as I arrived in yet another town. I had been completely distracted from any brief happiness, and everything felt marginally doomy.

Scuffed and dusty, Indians wrapped in blankets fell in the road as cars drove around them. Slumped under the eves of a hamburger stand, patronised by suspicious-looking characters, the grandson of an old Apache chief slugged back a half bottle of bourbon. Dodge trucks parked up, their head-lamps fell blindingly on my bike. In the back, tens of daughters of squaws had come for their evening takaway. As I munched warily on a jumbo burger a man wearing a white stetson hat introduced himself.

'The name's James, James McGawl and I'm the sheriff of this here town, pleased to meet you.' He shook my hand in much the same way a gorilla would have tried to wrench it off, but he looked friendly. 'You is drunk as a coot man,' he said to the chief, separating his words carefully , 'sober up and your wife will return.' Turning to me, he added, 'you know, these guys I have locked up in the jail and it is my belief that they sure do expect it. They're jus' not at all used to having any money. I guess they spend all their state cheques on the liquor, go ape-shit and I go ahead and lock them right up in that jail again.'

The dreadfulness of Magdalena made my head spin, all the motels had been raided for hard booze, banned because of the unruly behaviour of drunk Indians and so were closed for the night. As I was about to ride out of town, the sheriff invited me to sleep in his front garden which I gratefully accepted. He was spending the night with his girlfriend so I rolled out my bag under half a moon. Suffused with the manic and depressed sounds of a neurotic dog I dreamt fitfully.

Day 65: on Highway 60 to Socorro
Today all my will power has gone. I have no desire to carry on with the record. I

129

don't doubt that this schoolboy obsession to complete the ride is still there, but the journey has been in my thoughts for too long and I never think about anything else. It amazes me how quickly you accept a way of life to be normal. I am finding it difficult to concentrate and even harder to achieve the rhythm I need to get through each day. It's not easy to admit, but I think I'm homesick and I miss my Dad.

Pedalling briskly on Highway 60 I would soon turn north at Socorro and continue for 25 miles on Interstate 25 before bearing east again to Mountainair and Vaughn. Here families tended their geraniums and looked after granny on Sunday. To me the places were just names and every person a potential obstruction to the journey. I was presently immersed in a self interested egg-shell existence which eliminated all levels of life except for the one I was on. Yet if this journey was less obsessive, it would never have been undertaken.

It was illegal to cycle on most interstate roads but patrol cars passed me regularly and this time across America I wasn't given a single ticket. After two tablespoonfuls of rubberised scrambled egg and a not very 'genuine English muffin', the famous Macdonald's 99 cent breakfast, made me feel a little better. The 'ups and downs' are a part of any adventure, the regulation of which maybe *is* the adventure. But now the sun was shining, it was pleasantly warm and the road was becoming more friendly again. A couple of hours further along the road I saw a sign advertising coffee and doughnuts in the next layby. The Disarmed American Veteran Association were giving away refreshments in return for a small donation. Out of breath and sweaty, I sat down next to a man with one leg and enjoyed an unscheduled 20-minute stop.

'I saw men have bamboo spines stuck underneath fingernails to their first joint and when the finger could no longer bend, they just go and bend it until you hear the spine snap.' Smelling

strongly of chewed tobacco, the matted beard of this war veteran dipped into his coffee as he related his story. 'Aw heck, they called us baby killers when we got back. But you know these kids had grenades in their satchels and when they innocently walked into a group of soldiers they'd blow the whole lot up.'

Another fellow sat down opposite me, the skin on his face had pigmented white and brown and was loosely pinned, or so it seemed, onto half a nose and one ear.

'Napalm was probably dropped in his tank and he couldn't get out,' said the man with the beard, 'that or Agent Orange.'

Lifting an arm unsteadily to raise a cup to a place where his lips used to be, the man who had lost much of his face, sieved hot coffee through his teeth. Hands that no doubt had caressed tenderly the lovely features of a sweetheart or wife had melted and hardened, were now smooth and breakable like candlewax.

The road to Vaughn climbed through wasteland, suspicious and plain, only to drop by the odd settlement, quaint and broken down. Drooping musk thistles lined the route in their hundreds, crowded as they were with taller stalks of purple-tipped burdock. It had taken time but 'the rhythm' that I so needed to complete each day on schedule was now with me. I was never actually aware of the rhythm arriving but was conscious of a feeling of well being. The body was probably producing larger quantities of the hormone epinephrine, noted for the euphoria it gives when released. Concentration on the task in hand was now total and the wish to cycle around the world faster than anyone on earth allowed for no weakness. I felt an incredible sense of urgency and

for the first time in the USA began to believe the journey might end and that I wasn't going to be left in limbo for the rest of my life. It was only now, as I danced on the pedals, a picture slowly began to form in my head of New York and my having cycled across America to get there.

The road began to parallel a railway track just as six diesel locomotives grunted alongside pulling coupled container shipments to Santa Fe. There must have been 100 separate units that stretched a mile long and as I saw the driver look at me, I knew a race was on. As I waved, the train driver hooted as if to say 'keep up with me if you can,' and having the audacity to confront this metal monster, a little injured pride was at stake. I sprinted forward and as the bumpers clunked I sensed the train fractionally speed up. The engines thumped and thrust as I changed into a higher gear and edging closer to the driver's window, I then nosed a whisker's breadth beyond. I was in the lead and for a full hour we were locked in combat, after all, neither of us had anything better to do. Until it was no longer possible to see each other we raced, me gaining ground downhill the train catching up going uphill. The massive diesel turbines ranted and screamed and I panted and gasped. Occasional hillocks blocked our view and each time we emerged, I imagined I could see the whites of the eyes of the driver. Clenching my teeth, I climbed each short rise with a fury I had temporarily forgotten about. Every few minutes I slipped back a container or two, my legs ached and my chest was fit to burst. Although the fatigue of the long day had ground down most of my early morning anger, I had a little left to exorcize before the train was out of sight. I counted 106 separate trailers as

the last one at length pulled away from me. The driver had by now whistled to acknowledge his victory and I consoled myself with having been close to his clanking wheels for the whole second half of an afternoon. As the train petered off into the distance, I slowed down and my head sank to my elbows as I sat astride the bike exhausted. Sweat poured and dripped, and for a moment I trembled like an animal. I had without thinking incurred a cure for a hurt I couldn't actually find.

According to the map, I'd ridden 130 miles since this morning and had another 40 to go. Stopping a couple of times to fill up the water bottle I realised I'd climbed back up to 6,000 feet and was on a plateau that dipped and rolled. Hardly a car or truck passed me by as I ambled on with that never ending resignation which helped me complete another day. Resignation to a commitment is only one of several ways to ride a 170 miles every day. Switching on my 'walkman' was another way. Rarely making use of it, I suddenly felt an overwhelming desire to listen to music. I listened to 'Angie' from the Rolling Stones and felt soothed. It occurred to me that it wasn't the music that was important, more the need to engulf the din of my own thoughts. Hearing someone else's outpourings drooling into my ears negated the rattling vagaries prowling around my own head.

Ascending the last hill crest before the little town of Vaughn it was like riding into a painting. Fields of barley were gold and thorny sloe trees were white and grey.

skirts of Dalhart. Sitting outside a pizza parlour repairing yet another hole, the hissing sound of tyres deflating was, I decided, as much a part of today as were the blisters. Today the blisters were caused not by the cycling, but by the repairing of punctures. Whether I liked it or not, enforced stops allowed me to assimilate my surroundings; if only for a minute. I punctured at the start and was late for the bridge across the Jordan, and as I sheltered from the monsoon, I began to understand the God-forsaken sound of rain falling on corrugated huts all the way across India.

A few moments later I began to feel for the hole using the sensitive cornea of my eye. The rush of expelled air would make me blink and in this way I could locate the hole. I repaired all my punctures like this. As I sat alone in the darkness, a group of boys gathered around me. A couple of black boys sat astride wide motorbikes as a small group of girls clustered nearby. Seated in a bright red shiny clean Chevrolet, a young man was cool and collected as lads on foot winced and bitched. Grubby and sore, I was an obvious target at which to poke a little fun.

'Hey, what yer doin'?' A small slim boy shouted from the car. I wondered why I felt obliged to explain anything at all to these arrogant giggling youths that confronted me. I wanted to be courteous, but I was also wary.

'Hey, if you wanna get off with one of the chicks why don't you speak English to 'em, they'd jus' lerve you to do that.' The black guy who spoke smiled broadly, it would be a huge joke to them all if I offered the small blonde lady a lift home on the back of the bike.

'It would only be 4,500 miles love, and if you don't like cycling, then we can swim the last 3,000 if you like.'

'Suppose it would be easier to go

That night, after a quick meal in a twenty-four hour truckstop, I slept in the front garden of a church situated on a quiet mainstreet. Tomorrow evening I hoped to be in Dalhart, Texas. Another day and I will have cycled though another state of America.

The next day I arrived in Dalhart, my ankles and wrists were swollen. The blisters on my hands measured exactly the width of my handlebars and bled. I felt sick. *Day 66* was going as I might have expected.

As I skirted the small town of Tucumcari, everything started to go wrong. I punctured in Logan, and again in Nara Visa, 24 miles further on; I punctured several times beside fields of wheat and timothy grass; and I punctured twice on entering the out-around to her place, but it would be awfully tedious to have to meet the folks.'

The holes in the tube were almost microscopic and I was having trouble locating them. Why I should puncture so often all of a sudden was a puzzle, particularly as I'd ridden the length of Italy without one. Certainly after these past two days I was faster at repairing punctures than before. The time I took from the moment I heard the air hiss, to repairing the trouble and mounting the bike again, was eight minutes and forty-two seconds. I wondered if this too could be a world record, if so I shall ask the *Guinness Book of Records* to file it beside the '80 Day' entry under 'Cycling Endurance'. Only then, protruding from the inside of the tyre, did I spot the smallest of prickly spines. It was a 'sticker' from a spiny plant that grew in profusion here only to be blown across the road by a capricious wind.

'Hey, where was the last time you lerved a girl really close,' the black youth paused, 'you know what I mean,' and with ivory teeth that could have chewed somebody's head off, he laughed and made his pals laugh too. I didn't answer straightaway because I was so pleased with my discovery and wiped the inside of the tyre clean of any leftover spines.

'Calcutta,' I said after a moment, and at that, he obviously didn't know what to say, and I carried on repairing the innertube, my thumb and fingers stuck together with half a tube of glue.

Such was my gift of conversation that evening, I found myself without company. The blonde lady thought I was obtuse, so it was no use 'speaking English' to her. Placing the innertube

under the tyre and the wheel into the frame, I recalled one of very few things worth remembering in my days at school. A Japanese haiku I wrote was published in the school magazine, it read; 'Surrounded by friends, I look around, and find myself alone.' Nothing has changed, I am still alone. Grabbing a hamburger and a Coke from the store under whose verandah I was sitting, I cycled off having to settle for a nice warm hedge.

The following morning I decided to buy a new wheel with thick treaded tyres. My racing tyres had been selected for speed and it was ironic they should slow me so seriously now. Strapping the spare wheel to my front panniers I left Dalhart half a day behind schedule.

Dalhart was near the top end of a rectangle which stuck out of Texas and jutted into the Oklahoma Panhandle. Kansas bordered Oklahoma and that effectively allowed me to ride across three state borders in one day. Into and out of the wind and rain I ploughed on with my own private battle. New York was fixed in my mind as solid as the highway I was riding on. There were ten days left to cover 1,700 miles. For 15 hours I laboured along roads oily with yellow mechanical diggers, widening and straightening. As trees stood in file waiting to be torn out of the ground, fields of thick headed wheat wavered in a breeze that blew me east to Liberal.

Little things started to go wrong on the bike so come the next day, I wasn't able to leave Liberal until I'd carried out a few repairs. The bike had long since lost its youthful sparkle, not unlike its rider. Ralph Miller's Bike and Hobby shop replaced my newly acquired wheel with brand new racing tyres and I was told punctures would be fewer once I'd left the Mid West.

Ninety miles down on the most pessimistic schedule I rode with such fury as to remember nothing of *Day 68* except that it rained. *Day 69* became real only as I pedalled into El Dorado that evening, 350 miles east of Liberal. Several small eye capilliaries had broken due to grit and strain, and corneas, once white and bright, were red like pools of blood.

Parking my bike inside the foyer of the Sirloin Stockade steakhouse I sat down to as much salad as I could eat. After a bowl of steaming chicken soup, I munched through a plate of maize and celery followed by a small leg of lamb and half a pound of lipsmacking Stilton. At that point a couple of fellows asked if they could join me at my table, although there were numerous tables free, I could hardly refuse. One was heavily built and sported a moustache whilst the other man was fair and delicate, wearing excruciatingly zappy red shorts. They watched me eat and slurp more soup as the waiters were being particularly attentive, when the man with the moustache spoke,

'I'm the manager of this place and this is my friend,'

'They said I could eat as much as I wanted,' I blurted, 'I hope you don't mind, but they did say...'

'No, no it's not that, 'he said, a little taken back,' the girls told me what you were doing and your meal is already paid for. One of the lads will give you a spare bed for the night, I just wanted to say that what you are doing is really great.'

I was stunned. I felt like offering profuse thanks but knew it wasn't necessary. As they got up and left, every facility the restaurant could offer would be made available to me. Not for the first time, I was amazed by the generosity of American people. When, last year, I cycled 10,000 miles around the coast of Britain, I was honoured with one solitary act of hospitality. A little Italian café owner opposite the railway station in Littlehampton gave me a bag of fish and chips.

Within the hour I was tucked up in a nice warm bed gazing dreamily at the flickering of an old wrought iron street-lamp. Its reflection in the shiny road was interrupted only by browning sycamore leaves blowing in a breeze, a leftover from the day. In the corner of the room by the window, a fragile metal stand supported a white china hand basin. In the middle of the basin lay a bar of soap smelling of thyme. Close by softly washed linen towels, stood an ornate Victorian jug, old and cracked. The starched white bed sheets were stiff and creaky. They creaked when I moved and creaked when I remained quite still. Staring up to a cobwebby ceiling, it was obvious there hadn't been a lick of paint around these parts since the days long past. This house, with its hand polished floorboards and well rubbed doorknobs was the very one I imagined Mr and Mrs Lincoln to have lived in. Winnowed of all but the day's events I closed my eyes to sleep.

Day 71: El Dorado Springs

At 3 a.m. it's wet and cold, spitting rain blinds me and I am soaked to the skin. Am on the verge of panicking. So far to go and so little time. Don't know what to do. Am tired and getting a little emotional. Must keep a grip of myself, remain calm. I can make New York in eight days. I have to.

As the gulf between the dark heavens and the far off horizon grew wider the rain began to cease. I had pedalled through most of the night and shook with cold as I sat down in a small wooden café and ordered breakfast.

Sodden and miserable, it seemed a pattern had been set for the rest of the journey. Standing in front of an open fire, dripping and steaming, trapped rain formed rivulets down my anorak.

Breakfast arrived, fried eggs, bacon and hash browns with lashings of tomato sauce. I ate ravenously. Taking out my diary and map of America I began to work out the most direct route home. Now I was in Missouri, a rolling land of red roofed verandahs under which old men sat, drawing smoke greedily from warm bowls of well thumbed pipes. If I continued cycling 170 miles per day I should reach Edgar Springs that night. Tomorrow I should be well past the nightmare of St Louis. The last time I was there, I was nearly killed by a speeding lorry oblivious to my whereabouts. *Day 73* would place me firmly in Columbus, Ohio, my having crossed the state of Indiana. Assuming the wind didn't turn against me, *Day 74* would end in Wheeling, West Virginia. Three days and 600 miles later, I would be standing next to some New Yorker leaning against the World Trade Towers, swatting flies.

As I cycled throughout the day it seemed that it wasn't so long ago that the eastern seaboard was something I could only vaguely understand. Now New York itself was in the forefront of my mind, and I was trying to decide quite where the journey was going to end. To end the journey there would make sense, but a cicumnavigation of the world wouldn't be complete until I actually arrived in my home country. If I decided to end the journey in London and not Manchester, where I started, it would not be a major compromise. Now, however, my thoughts were focused on New York. Saying to myself, 'I must get to New York' was the understatement of my life. The success of the journey had become more important than I could have imagined. Yet, as my success is to me all important, so my failure would be devastating. Through the night and through the rain I continued to cycle. The drizzle had lasted ten hours and by daybreak my thoughts were as disjointed as broken glass. I was tired beyond reason. My eyes began to close; and fighting off the spray of the trucks, I wrapped myself in my cape to curl up like a dog on the side of the road.

Day 72: 8 a.m. On the road to St Louis
The concentration is intense. I think of each day as the goal of my life. The rhythm is coming along beautifully but I do need sleep. I sleep on the side of the road. My legs cramp up badly. I lie in the drizzling rain, warmed by my own body heat, it doesn't feel so bad.

I became increasingly aware of a certain savagery in adventure which appeals to the primitive instincts in human nature, and on reaching the outskirts of St Louis, I tensed as if ready for battle. The freeway was awash with the rush hour flood of traffic, weaving between houses of every manner and character. As the road narrowed, houses closed in around me and glancing with the impunity travellers are often afforded, I saw the pourers of coffee and makers of meals in the rapidly dimming light. It became obvious people living on the banks of the Mississippi were preparing to sit down for their tea. From the outside looking in, people being fed and watered looked warm and cosy. As windows steamed up with the hot breath of the feast, I began to concentrate on the task of traversing St Louis.

The last time I crossed St Louis, I was a fingernail distance away from being killed. Then, as now, the wind of the trucks pressed me hard against freeway railings. Without any remorse, back trailers scratched my elbows as

they passed me and if my reflex action had been slow, my arm would have been ripped out of its socket. I had hoped it wouldn't happen again. I also hoped I shouldn't puncture. But, in fact, I punctured entering the city limits and I punctured across the Missouri. I punctured in East St Louis and I punctured across the Mississippi. Again, the city of St Louis had unwittingly been unkind to me. As the trucks scorched and strained, climaxing on the bridge crossing America's greatest river, I was riding in the wake of something infinitely less fragile. As a hard sun slipped unnoticed in the midst of the skyline, the city had at least been crossed and, heading off into the night, I breathed a sigh of relief.

Day 72: Midnight and I don't know where I am

Only hours ago I had an idea I was journeying through St Louis. Now all I know is that I am lying on the side of a road some time either side of Day 72. *One truck after another thunders past and my mind is numbed by the noise. Surrounded by the lights and the horns and the scattering of grit, I feel so dreadfully alone. Never in my life have I felt as I do now; that in a paltry 72 days I should respond to my feelings with such panic. For me, the mechanics of ordinary life now work in an entirely different way than when I began this journey. Then, I lived and worked in a situation where there was little unknown. Now it is raining. I wipe my nose, warm my hands, shiver in the night and move as little as possible to minimise the effect of each muscle spasm as they come and go. Too fatigued to find appropriate shelter, I crouch in an old concrete pipe. The exhaustion of each day's effort is making it difficult for me to think. How I should like to write in my diary that 'the adventure is progressing well and that I* *confidently expect to be in New York very soon.' Instead I go on tediously about my anxiety and my fear of being alone. Too near, the harsh tragic sound of a police siren wails as I comfort myself with the perverse notion that I'm not really alone. Do most people most often feel this way too? Aching, I sense the adventure has become frivolous.*

Day 73 and I cycle from Casey to Indianapolis to Centreville to Columbus. *Day 74* comes and goes as I cycle for yet another 16 hours. Here and there I weave. Zanesville, Cambridge, and in and out of the Ozarks, finally entering Wheeling on the northern edge of West Virginia, I was close to New York. After being on the road for 74 days, it was less than three days away. Soon the journey would be over. Not yet having consulted the map in detail, I guessed there be approximately 400 miles left to ride. As I stood by the road waiting for someone to pass so I could ask for the directions across town, it hurt, but now I could laugh. All I had to do was ride through the night and the crossing of the Tuscarora mountains in the loveliness of Pennsylvannia could be mine for half a day. It was only a matter of time, a very very small portion of what has gone before. I asked the way to New York.

'New York,' said the man with a tangled black beard.

'Yes,' I said, 'Is it far?'

'Far, on that thing,' and he pointed at my bike, 'you gotta be outta yer tree boy, it's on the other side of the world. This is a joke, huh?'

'No,' I told him, it was not a joke, I had cycled around the world and I was in rather a hurry.

'Not so fast boy,' he said and looking like a Hell's Angel he took a deep breath and his leather jacket creaked.

'Maybe yer lyin' maybe yer not, but it's a darn good story and I want yer to meet some pals of mine.' Picking up my bike and carrying it across the road and into a bar was his way of insisting I have a drink. One little drink could hardly do any harm.

'Boys, we got a fella here all the way from England and he's jus' gone an' bicycled here from 'er,' he paused and turned to whisper to me, 'where did yer say yer came from?'

'Around the world,' I said.

'Yea,' he said scratching an armful of tattoos which came alive in the red neon of the bar. 'Yea, he's jus' gone an' come from around the world and he's nearly bin' round it on his bi-cycle.'

There was a silence and an embarrassment. Within this sad and dingy corner of the world, I looked down at the floor. They would not understand. There was a shuffling of feet and several of the men in the middle of ordering a drink looked at me. In the far corner of the bar someone clapped their hands slowly. It sounded like the derision of a slow hand-clap. No one was drinking now, and another fellow began to bring his hands together. The bar clapped and now so did the far corner. The pool table stomped its feet, and everyone seated began to bang their glass. Slowly, together, a chorus line of heavy, beery, embattled Pittsburg steel-workers celebrated the near conclusion of my very own world record with a style and dignity I thought would be hidden in the neon. The bar was gently in turmoil and everyone shook

139

their head. If the journey could have finished at that very moment, it could not have been given a better ending than such appreciation from these men.

'Have a beer,' someone shouted.

'Have another,' and someone else threw me a bottle.

I had another and another and another.

It was dark inside and it was dark outside and as I began to notice the rings of old beer on the bar top, I had an idea something was amiss when I found I could hardly stand up.

'Have another beer,' they shouted, so I did.

A leg went and I grappled furiously for a moment hanging on to a chair without letting go of my glass. An arm went, but due to a little good fortune my left leg had returned to its more usual position, preventing a premature end to the evening. The big man had arms that were bigger than my legs and his legs were the size of my waist.

'Yer must be mad little feller,' and putting his arm around me he proceeded to drink most of the remainder of his beer by holding the glass with his teeth. What beer didn't end up in his belly, dribbled down his chin on to my head. I was about to explain that there was no actual dividing line between sanity and madness, that the one flowed into the other and that you would not know if such a measure of madness had been reached, but someone gave me another beer. I could drink no more. In the back of my mind there was somewhere I still had to go, but as I'd long forgotten quite where I was, schedules and bicycle rides would have to be remembered. That was it, bicycles. I said this to my Hell's Angel friend and he laughed.

'New York,' I said, 'what was I saying about New York?'

'Yer said yer were bi-cycling around the world boy.' My God, he was right.

'I must go, I said, 'or it'll all be for nothing.'

'Have another drink.' I thanked him kindly but said no. I grabbed hold of my bike and leant on it, after which I wheeled it to the door.

'Goodbye,' I said, 'and thank you.' The door was opened allowing me fresh breathfuls of cool night air. I wrapped one of my legs over the bike and grabbed hold of the handlebars. I had an idea that if I turned right out of the bar I would still be going east, but I wasn't sure. As he held me up, I could feel the tangled beard in my hair and with a mighty shove I was sent on my way. For a moment I steered, and then for a moment I didn't. Cruising in a northerly direction somewhere in the same path of an oncoming lampost, I came briefly to my senses and prior to hitting what I would normally avoid, remembered my final option. I closed my eyes.

Opening my eyes, I focused on an unfamiliar sight. I had a vague idea I

141

should have been studying the road in detail, but my Hell's Angel friend placed a cup of coffee by my side.

'Yer gone an hell knocked yerself clean out, I had to carry yer to my place myself and boy did you sleep well.'

I closed my eyes and smiled, it was the following morning, I was 12 hours behind on my schedule with less than three days to New York, the absurdity was complete. The craziest of scene changes was now to be enacted. I got up, dressed, offered my warmest thanks and said goodbye.

It was *Day 75* and I rode with the devil inside me. I rode south of Pittsburg and on to Mount Pleasant. I brushed past Somerset and bathed in the colours of a garden landscape that smelt of haystacks and horses and sounded with the happy shrieks of children playing. All day I cycled until dark. It rained and it hailed and occasionally it was dry. Here and there I ate what I could hold as I rode. Almost without a thought, carefree or otherwise, I powered the bike up the crest of every hill and free-wheeled fast and furiously until I climbed again. I was on my way up the Allegheny Plateau in the Appalachian Mountains, then I would be on my way down. If there wasn't a meaning to this pattern, there was at least a consistency. On the night of *Day 75* I slept on the back porch of somebody's house in a tiny town called Everett. There are only so many ways in which a journey can put over the meaning of tiredness. My diary is blank, my thoughts squeezed dry. So I slept for three hours and I continued on to *Day 76*.

On *Day 76* I continue on to McConnellsburg and Chambersburg and I reach the top of the Tuscarora Mountains and I then descend to Shippensburg and to Harrisburg and across the Susquehanna river. So I eat and drink and cycle, get lost and ask the way. So I follow the river to Lebanon and to Reading, I push and push and reach Allentown and Bethlehem. I am so tired yet I have time only to sleep for three hours. It is *Day 77* and I have 100 miles yet to do. Tonight I fly from New York to London. Tomorrow, in London, on *Day 78*, the journey will end.

10 · RACING FOR HOME

All around me, lorries of the East Coast of the USA coughed and spluttered, flooding into New York like some tidal bore. They raged and hurled themselves forward as if I wern't there. I felt a fairly dispensable commodity on the run-in to New York. Around the sweeping bends of this eight lane highway I stood on top of a raised concrete platform that separated the road from everything else. I had only three miles to go and it would be a pity if I were flattened by a lorry so near to the end of the journey.

Around the bends, I rode slowly with more caution than I'd used on any other section of the ride. Any moment I would see what I'd been looking for these past two and a half months and approximately 13,000 miles. My heart pounded with exitement. There it stood, in the distance, wavering a little in the haze, the George Washington Bridge, the final landmark on my journey.

There was a press call for me in New York. The *Daily Express* had flown two reporters out to meet me. There was a satellite link up to the BBC, and later that afternoon I appeared on *The Bill Boggs Show*.

As I wheeled my bike into the television studio, which was large and impressive, someone then led me to the make-up room. There were two other guests invited that day, one of the fattest men in the world and one of the shortest women from the East Coast. I was the 'special guest'.

As the make-up artist powdered my cheeks, a man swathed in the bandages of an Egyptian mummy sat down next to me so he could be unwrapped. Sitting next to him, a couple of girls with pink and yellow hair turned out to be men. The journey had almost ended and I was back into the weird world.

'Nick, you're on,' and a floor assistant took me back into the studio. Each time Bill Boggs took a break a film was shown and a comedian cajoled the audience to keep on laughing with a few inane jokes.

'And now ladies and gentlemen, here comes Mr Bill Boggs...'

The audience screamed for him.

'Thank you. No, stop it, you're all too much!' Bill kept saying, wringing his hands, laughing nervously. 'And now ladies and gentlemen, included in today's 'Strange But True Fact File,' a man who's just bicycled around the world in sixty-eight days, Mr Dick Sanders...'

The audience screamed for me. But then they had just got over the shock of seeing one of the fattest men in the world.

'Dick, this is really an amazing voyage, you know its so incredible I jus' don't believe it!' He looked at the audience to see if they believed it, he nodded his head from side to side with a grin and they agreed with Bill. 'Tell all of our lervly people what it was like to bicycle around the whole of the world.'

'It was great,' I said grinning.

'It was great, ladies and gentlemen, did you here that?'

Somebody in front of the audience raised a blackboard, which was presumably marked with the word 'laugh,' because that was what they did.

The audience screamed for me again.

Bill looked at me gravely. 'But of course, this re-mar-kable adventure of yours was much much more than just a bicycle ride, huh? I mean did your backside get sore?'

The blackboard went up again and the audience roared with laughter.

'No seriously folks,' Bill said, as if pleading with the audience for calm, 'this is an epic ride.' He turned to me again making sure he was looking over my shoulder at the appropriate camara. There was a momentary pause and a look of seriousness. 'You must be a changed man?'

'Yes,' I said, nodding.

'Yes, what?' Bill looked nervous, I was not the predictable guest he was used to interviewing.

'Yes, I got thinner!'

Up went the blackboard again and the audience screamed for me.

A couple of minutes later I was in a busy New York street and as the show hadn't finished, Bill would still be laughing nervously and the audience would have forgotten me already.

The reporters from the *Express* were people I could better understand, because, to borrow an American expression, 'they goofed'. I was to pose for the paper with the Statue of Liberty in the background. Jumping onto the Stratton Island Ferry we set sail, camaras to the ready. As we got closer to this awe-inspiring iron lady, we saw with dismay, from head to foot she was covered in scaffolding. Still she welcomed me, and quietly I said hello to her. Instead, we turned around to make use of the famous Manhatten skyline. I had waited so long and journeyed so far to see one of the most famous skylines in the world. It was rendered invisible by the smog. This was a delightful little farce, to fly 3,000 miles for a photograph of me against a background of scaffolding and smog. We settled for a shot of me shaking hands with a New York policeman.

As the ferry sailed back to port, the shapes of the Empire State Building and World Trade Towers could at last be seen, they soared magnificently.

Friends had flown here to greet me and in the Covent Garden area of town I wandered around in a daze. I had slept well for eight hours in the last two and a half days and I had cycled 400 miles. The most arduous and debilitating journey I had ever undertaken in my life was effectively over.

In the early evening I was driven to Newark Airport and boarded a Virgin Airways flight to London. I travelled first class and could drink as much champagne as I wished. As I sat looking out of an aircrafts window into blackness, I felt suddenly tired and pensive and already sad. The journey had ended.

In the hotel I had received three letters. From my father, from Vivienne, my PA and friend, and one slightly soiled from Syria. It was a beautiful letter and would undoubtedly be misinterpreted. I didn't care.

My Dear Nick Sanders,

If fate has separate between our bodies but our friendship is lasting even if we are different in languages. My dear friend it is true that we have met only once in our life, I feel that I know you many ago. So my wish to see you is always increasing thus we have to keep our friendship and make it more journeyful against the time which usually eats everything beautiful. Finally I wish that you were happy in your worldly journey and in your life I hope that we will meet together soon. Please send me the rememberence we had together and the pictures of your family. My best compliments to you.

Your Sincere friend,

Husain Al Hasan.

So the plane began to descend and the watery roofs of England could at last be seen. I was nervous, visibly shaking. A large contingent of sponsors, PR people, agents, press and perhaps a few friends would be waiting in a room specially set aside for my arrival.

The plane touched down and the two journalists escorting me home wished me luck. How I longed for the anonymity of the vast plains of the Mid-West. There I could hide. Recognition of my achievement excited me, but it also mortified me. In front of all these people I was on public display and I had become a very private person. Ushered quickly through immigration and customs I was whisked through the arrival hall to a set of swing doors. On the other side of these doors I could hear the murmur of a party. I took a deep breath, in the same way as might an actor on the evening of his first night.

As I pushed my bike into the room,

everyone erupted into applause. Flash lights blinded me, champagne corks hit the ceiling, everybody was smiling. I was introduced to one journalist after another, the story had to be told. As I turned this way then that, someone took another photograph. I was determined not to be emotional, but a tear crept into the corner of my eye. Dad would be waiting for me in Glossop where he said I'd be certain of a rapturous welcome. But now, both at the same time, I was ecstatically happy and a little sad. The journey had ended successfully, the pain was over, but I wondered for a moment how the rest of my life could compare with this elation?

In that moment, I suddenly felt the answer to the question why had I ever undertaken this reckless, painful and pointless journey. I remembered once reading a story about a Bushman in Southern Africa:

A Bushman child, drinking from a clear waterhole, saw in the shimmering surface the reflection of a beautiful bird, the most beautiful thing he had ever seen. But looking upward, he knew that the bird had already gone. The boy decided he had to follow and find it. He sought it throughout his adolescence and throughtout his youth, but was always one step behind his quarry. In his old age the hunter reached the lower slopes of Mount Kilimanjaro and was told that the bird had been seen high up on the snowy summit. The old man, climbed labouriously up the mountainside.

There, in the equatorial snow and ice, all his strength gone, he saw nothing but emptiness. He lay down to wait for death. He had been lucky enough to find beauty once, and in his heart he had never lost it. As he closed his eyes for the last time, he called on the name of his mother, who had given him such a wonderful and joyous life. And as he stretched out his arms in a final gesture, his open hands upturned, down from the sky came a solitary feather and settled in one hand.

Nick presenting Princess Anne with a cheque for £50,000 for Save the Children Fund. The money was raised by *SPAR's* fundraising efforts.